Upside Down Debate

Upside Down Debate

A DEEPER WHY TO PERSUASION

ISAIAH & BETSY MCPEAK

Ethos Publications LLC ● Austin, TX

Contents

Introduction

You can't learn to debate by reading a book. Debate is still a skill. But you can't *master* everything debate offers without some books—and not just this one.

We wrote this book because of what debate has done in our lives. Debate has forever changed the way we think and make decisions. It's like putting on glasses after years of looking at a fuzzy world. We wrote this book because we know that debate can do the same in your life. We also wrote this book because of the misconception that debating means being argumentative and talking the most.

True rhetoric, what we call upside-down debate, is different: Deserving to speak means listening first, thinking second, and possibly, maybe, opening one's mouth.

Although just reading this book won't make you a great debater, we hope to provide the tools and patterns of thought that help you get the most out of... well... life.

What Does Upside Down Mean?

In a world where people too often think of communication as a means of domination, getting what you want, and looking good, rhetoric is dead. **Upside Down Debate** is our attempt to train a generation to learn debate differently: advising audiences to make great decisions, deep listening, seeking to make others whole through conflict resolution, and persuasion that ultimately removes self as an obstruction of ideas worth sharing.

In the Upside Down world, rhetoric isn't about "sounding good," it's about thinking well first and earning the right to speak well second.

Upside Down is inspired by Rabbi Yeshua's message to live a life differently, in the Kingdom of God here and now alongside everyone else. For debaters, this means:

- valuing listening over speaking
- relish creatively analyzing an argument, while never advocating a position with which you do not agree (most people think you must make this compromise to debate; we do not)
- loving the audience more than self
- hoping for the best result, even if your opponent is the one who has it
- cutting no corners, going through the narrow gate of research, discipline, and intellectual honesty
- turning conflict into healing
- not proving "my side," but connecting audiences with higher ideals and sharing the experience
- choosing to view listeners as ends, rather than means to your own ends

We also call this light-side rhetoric, an allusion to the Jedi and Sith, who use power for others (light) or self (dark). In this, we invite you to join Plato and Aristotle in the ancient battle against the Sophists, those abusers of rhetoric who glory in persuading audiences of that which they do not believe.

Who is this Mysterious "I"?

You will find that many chapters are written in first person. We believe storytelling makes learning more fun, even if it costs some grammar points. Sometimes "I" is Betsy, sometimes "I" is Isaiah, and sometimes "I" is even a special guest.

Acknowledgments

Isaiah's Acknowledgments

Where to start? I am especially thankful for my debate students, from whom I have always learned more than I teach. I especially appreciate the debaters that taught me to be a national-class coach, that original core group of team policy debaters at Vector debate club in Purcellville, VA: Lydia Bode, Peter Voell, Dan Pugh, Rebekah Kintzing, James Kintzing, Chloe Snyder, Sarah Snyder, Anna Snyder, and Drew Chambers.

The mentors and people who invested in my life, guiding me to always give back and coach, have all shaped me in more ways than they will ever know. These mentors include Betsy McPeak, David McPeak, Wayne Cameron, Lisa Alexander, and Dr. Jim Tallmon. Sorry for those gray hairs!

Thanks to all the debaters of APEX (Always Pursuing Excellence), an amazing three-year project organized by Gary Downing. You have all become my lifelong friends, and are the reason I decided to finish this book.

The amazing staff at Ethos are the ones who helped start this book so many times, and are my lifelong colleagues in all kinds of crazy projects. Thanks especially to Abbey Lovett, Tim Snyder, Drew Chambers (again), Josiah McPeak, Patrick Shipsey, and Ty Harding.

Thanks to Michael Farris for believing in me in June of 2004 – it made a lifetime of a difference. And lastly, thank you past debate partners, especially Blake Bozarth, Kawika Vellalos, and the late Emily Roe.

Betsy's Acknowledgments

Fifteen years ago our two oldest sons kick-started my first debate club by saying, "We want to debate." Before I even located a debate text, I stood in front of a group of educators in O'Fallon, Illinois and recruited 33 high school students to join us in our first club. As in most of the good adventures of my life, someone was upstream to offer encouragement, and someone was downstream to motivate me onward.

Upstream was Carol Wetherhill and Debbie Whitehair to answer weekly panic emails about tournaments, debate theory and partnerships. Downstream were our own sons and 31 other students that I stayed one week ahead of in my forensics knowledge that first year.

Being a debate coach has both clarified and stimulated my own thinking. Thank you to David, my ever-faithful husband who shared a vision of the value of debate and spent hours and hours discussing debate with me, and relating it to real life.

Thank you to all four sons, Jonathan, Isaiah, Josiah and Samuel, and all of my other students along the way who made teaching and coaching debate one of the best experiences in my life.

Special thanks to Isaiah for how creatively he envisions amazing projects and spurs me on, providing clarity and keeping the focus on what is really important in debate, and in life.

Chapter 1. Why Debate?

Have you ever been in a conversation that went like this?

> Them: I think we should dramatically expand the amount of immigrants who can legally enter our country, because it would foster innovation to have more minds coming in.

> You: That's probably a good reason for a high skill visa program, but not to allow more of all types of immigrants.

> Them: But that assumes it is good to have more highly skilled people in the country.

> You: I thought that's what you were saying.

> Them: No, I was just referring to immigrants overall.

You: Right, and I'm saying you should look at just high-skilled people to bring that innovation.

Them: See, now you're assuming they are more innovative. How do you know they actually are?

You: ARGGHHHHH

Or perhaps you more often have conversations like this one:

Mom: You need to clean your room—I don't like seeing it so messy all the time. Plus you keep losing things. Nobody will trust you with big things if you can't be trusted with the little things, like being organized.

You: Actually, I am getting quite a few big things done right now. I'm on a robotics team and have a part time job.

Mom: That's not the point.

You: I was just logically answering your claim.

Mom: ARGHH. Don't talk back!

You'd be misunderstanding debate to think you should keep arguing in either situation. Neither are arguments. Neither are debates.

In the first conversation, the person clearly cares more about you being wrong than about having a real discussion.

In the second conversation, Mom's point is that you just need to clean your room. Your mom gives you a general principle with implications as an example, but you attack the example and not her overall point. You can almost always refute common sense with a particular example, but common sense is still usually right. Both of you end up frustrated, because you changed the topic to the example, and in the end, your mom changed the topic from cleaning your room to respect towards her.

In both cases you disagreed with the other person to begin with, but they changed their point of view along the way, adding confusion to the mix. Often, someone who feels cornered does not want to admit what happened, because they were actually out of arguments (or out of ways to explain it at the moment). We will spend more time later discussing how to help those you are debating trust you enough to admit to some agreement.

For now, we are making this point: when the topic of the debate shifts during the debate, it becomes frustrating and ineffective.

In formal debate we avoid that problem. That's because **the structure of debate establishes the framework of the debate, the types of arguments to be used, and the method of evaluation**. In competitive debates, a topic is assigned in each round. The topic *does not change* during the round. This clarifies what each side is arguing. If one side switches their position, they will lose. The format insures that each side gets to present their arguments fairly. Lastly, an impartial judge weighs the arguments presented to determine who wins the debate, so that if one side does switch their position, it will affect the outcome of the debate. Debate attempts to set up a forum where participants can weigh all the elements of the arguments.

Debate is all about decision-making.

The purpose of debate is to learn the principles and execution of an oral argument: demonstrating why some decisions are better than other decisions. You will learn how to communicate to a wide array of individuals, testing out arguments and phrasing to see what works when. You will grapple with controversy.

What Tools Are Needed for This Activity?

- Critical thinking—relating more than one domain (or subject) of knowledge to another in order to recommend a decision.
- Reasoned exchange of ideas—handling disagreement as a different perspective worthy of discussion on the merits, not as a personal challenge.
- Discrimination—learning which ideas apply and which are irrelevant to the *decision*, even if seemingly related to the *subject*.
- Communication—helping other humans see your perspective through their eyes.
- Listening—engaging with and processing the written and spoken thoughts of others, taking notes to track the development of arguments over time. (Later in this chapter we will introduce *flowing*—the note-taking method most commonly used in debate.)
- Perspective – understanding another position or point-of-view, even if you do not agree with it. Understanding the other side of the argument will help you form compelling and effective responses.

Debate Holds Lifelong Rewards

Debate is not a sport for geeks who can't play football. But sometimes we have seen it pursued that way! Debate provides the tools and patterns of thought that help you get the most out of... well... life.

The school of debate we hope to share is the one that we've seen leave a lifelong positive mark upon its students – including ourselves. Debate has helped us to present to global CEOs, speak well on television, train underprivileged youth in public speaking, start or participate in significant movements, write influential books, help governments make better decisions, give sports coaches better words to say, have better relationships, get more out of education, be better parents, and generally live richer lives.

Debate is deeply connected to life because the principles of communication that make you an effective debater are the very same principles that make you an effective decision-maker in real life. It is just one part of an exploration into all that rhetoric has to offer, but it is the most tangible—easy to start, valuable to try, and rewarding at every new level of mastery.

Debate Can Move Everyone Toward Good

Debate is about much more than the confidence to stand in front of an audience and articulate relevant points. When pursued through disciplined thinking, debate can provide confidence that you:

- have considered every angle
- are truly recommending good reasons for a good decision
- can research the right information or ask the right questions
- are able to defuse hostile conflict
- can see the reasonableness of someone who disagrees with you
- are able to anticipate objections
- have tools to resist empty persuasion and rhetoric
- can think both logically and analogically, when planning and in real-time

- know your strengths and limitations in analysis
- are familiar with the range of emotion, rationality, and biases of humans
- see through distracting semi-important facts to identify the crux (*stasis*)
- can discriminate between motive, fact, and individual personalities
- are an effective listener
- understand the appropriate tone and language for changing situations
- have virtuous habits of intellectual honesty and critical self-reflection
- are capable at providing greater wisdom and clarity to any situation, or recognizing that you have nothing of value to add

What has debate done for us? It has taught us to make better decisions. As corny as it sounds, debate has made us into better people: in business, in self-education, in classrooms, in relationships, as parents, and as participants in any process.

But debate is not only about you. Your words, research, interactions with opponents, ideas, how you treat others, and internal thoughts all affect others. Many events that changed the course of history were seeded, instigated, or even directly caused by rhetoric. Consider some of the following famous words. Even if you can't guess the source or occasion of these powerful words, see how many you recognize:

1. 'Will he not fancy that the shadows which he formerly saw are truer than the objects which are now shown to him?"
2. "Therefore, whatever you want men to do to you, do also to them."
3. "To no one will we sell, to no one will we refuse or delay right or justice."
4. "Hence today I believe that I am acting in accordance with the will

of the Almighty Creator: 'by defending myself against the Jew, I am fighting for the work of the Lord.'"

5. "We hold these truths to be self-evident, that all men are created equal, that they are endowed by their Creator with certain unalienable Rights, that among these are Life, Liberty and the pursuit of Happiness."

6. "We the people of the United States, in order to form a more perfect Union, establish justice, insure domestic tranquility, provide for the common defense, promote the general welfare, and secure the blessings of liberty to ourselves and our posterity, do ordain and establish this Constitution for the United States of America."

7. "Keep your friends close, your enemies closer."

8. "... government of the people, by the people, for the people ..."

9. "City on a Hill"

10. "Men are born free and remain free and equal in rights."

11. "Now and then the workers are victorious, but only for a time. The real fruit of their battles lies, not in the immediate result, but in the ever expanding union of the workers."

12. "Et tu, Brute"

13. "I have a dream."

14. "That's one small step for a man, one giant leap for mankind."

15. "Axis of Evil"

16. "... ask not what your country can do for you — ask what you can do for your country."

17. "...I shall return."

Sources:

1. Plato's Cave, from The Republic

2. Jesus' Golden Rule

3. Magna Charta

4. Mein Kampf, by Adolf Hitler

5. The U.S. Declaration of Independence

6. The U.S. Constitution

7. Sun Tzu – *The Art of War*

8. Abraham Lincoln's Gettysburg Address

9. Any of the following: Sermon on the Mount; John Winthrop of early America; J.F. Kennedy; Ronald Reagan

10. Declaration of the Rights of Man (France)

11. Communist Manifesto

12. Julius Caesar by Shakespeare

13. Martin Luther King, Jr.

14. Neil Armstrong

15. George W. Bush

16. John F. Kennedy

17. Douglas MacArthur

Even if you can think of major historical events not associated with significant historical rhetoric, that does not mean the influence of rhetoric ended. How is it that any event is of major significance? Because—through rhetoric—history is repeated over and over, passed down in stories and accounts. Rhetoric is the conduit of the significance of historical events, passing the importance on to people in the future.

Debate Can Be Evil

Sophist: A person who reasons with clever but fallacious arguments.
Oxford Dictionaries

When pursued as a discipline attached to the ancient principles of Classical Rhetoric—in the school of Plato and Aristotle, who condemned the Sophists—debate is learned as a dangerous weapon.

Sophistry: Emphasizing Winning Over Truth

It can be a surgeon's scalpel and move others towards good, or a nine-tailed whip that accomplishes selfish ends. Thus, the discipline of debate we refer to in this book means the self-challenge of learning habits that are good through debate, rather than cultivating patterns that shape the soul towards manipulation, selfish dominance, and the desire to defeat other people.

> "What makes a man a 'sophist' is not his faculty, but his moral purpose."
> *Aristotle, The Art of Rhetoric (1355b 17)*

Think about it: what is more powerful than getting people to do or believe things? Rhetoric is far more effective than physical force in changing beliefs, and beliefs lead to action.

We have seen many great debaters accomplish incredible, meaningful things. We've also seen incredibly successful debaters use their skill for evil, self-paralysis*, and harm. Another difficult observation is that we've seen many debaters rely on a knack for debate and never pursue their potential, sometimes even after five or six years in the activity. **We wrote this book to help debaters choose the better path with debate, see its value and mechanics, and find practical ways to challenge self to the greatest heights of value rhetoric and debate can offer to you, and through you, to the world.**

> *****Self-paralysis** means to ask so many "analytical" questions of oneself that one is never sure enough to make a decision and act. So you end up in theoretical debates inside your head constantly. "You could think of it this way, or that way, or this other way," overanalyzing to the point of incapacitation.

Addressing What's Broken in Debate: Subject or Discipline?

Too often competitive debate students learn the language of debate and then live in the "debate world" throughout the season of their debate experience. Even the best debaters then have to *translate* debate language and theory into real life in order for debate to have any significant, long-term value. Competition is magnificent as a chance to practice rhetoric and decision-making many times in a row, with clear feedback and room to experiment. But *transference*—bringing that experience to the rest of life—is the challenge for every competitive debater to overcome.

> "Rhetoric has no subject matter of its own." *Aristotle*

There is an entire community of competitive debate at high school and college levels that has become disconnected from life. People spend eight years in competitive debate practicing concepts and skills with words, language, and values that makes debate a subject of its own. Sadly, this is precisely how debate digresses from the art of rhetoric and requires extra work from every debater to translate debate experience to the rest of life. That's a problem.

You've probably heard of foreign language programs that sell their product by claiming that you can skip the translation stage by learning the language *in* the language. Rather than your mind thinking in English and then translating into Swahili, good language programs just teach you Swahili in Swahili, skipping the translation stage. That's what we want to do with debate. We want to skip the translation stage from competitive debate to the real world. We want you to learn debate as rhetoric—a discipline, not a subject—through real-world thinking, words, concepts, and applications. So expect many analogies to business, relationships, everyday decisions, politics, and so on, as we learn the subjectless subject of rhetoric, through the lens of debate.

The Debater's Commitment

> On my honor I will do my best to wield the power of rhetoric always for the good of my fellow human, never as a means to victory or self-enrichment only. I promise never to treat my opponents in speech contests as means to ends, but always, as Kant says, as "potential members of the kingdom of ends." I will debate as a teacher, not a conqueror: Docere, Delectare, Movere (Latin for to teach, to delight, to move).

We urge you to adopt a mindset of the Debater's Commitment, inspired by Dr. James Tallmon, former professor of Rhetoric and Leadership at Patrick Henry College. If you've committed yourself to a life of communicating to move others towards the good, you are the type of person we hope to equip. If you're not, please go away.

Primum non nocere

On the one hand, you can join the Dark Side (classically, the Sophists), and learn to debate without regard for others, truth, or self-challenge. It is our hope that you join the light side, and challenge yourself to a higher standard, engage in the world of ideas, and use the force of rhetoric as a means to ends greater than your individual gain.

This book *will* help you in competitive debate—you can become a great debater. But that is not the end goal. This book aims to help you to learn debate in ways that make the world better. Take the plunge, challenge yourself, and join me in a lifetime of moving others towards good.

The Real Life Test

Decisions are made every day—in your own head, at the dinner table, with friends, in business, in politics, in family, in leadership—in everything you do. Debate assimilates your knowledge and forces you to practice thinking through decisions from more angles than you ever have, interacting with those who disagree with you. The only difference is that in real life the *format* is different, depending on when and where you are making decisions and who is listening.

Thus, a key principle of debate is what we call the **real life test**: when the "theory" of debate is in question, it ought to always be related to the equivalent principle in some other real life discipline.

So when a team argues, "you need to win all three of your harms to win this debate round," you can successfully argue "one good reason can be enough to validate change." Just because cost savings were not a good reason to stop eating out every day, the impact to personal health still stands as a reason to stop eating out every day. The same is true in policy decisions. Put your arguments through the real life test, and be ready with equivalent decisions in real life contexts.

You will also likely need to argue as to why the real life test is the appropriate method to weigh arguments. We devote an entire chapter to concepts of debating about the debate, which we call meta-debate. Suffice it for now to say that you do not "win" arguments just because you made the right ones—you have to justify arguments in order to persuade your audience which arguments are the deciding factors.

An Isaiah story...

In one round at a national championship in 2003, my partner and I were arguing against the team that won the whole tournament. Their case was to provide up to $15 billion in aid to Africa. We showed several reasons why this was a bad idea and why it would not work. Instead of focusing on the content of what we were saying, the team spent too much time arguing, "my opponents didn't show the link, brink, and impact to their disadvantages."At the time, we had no idea what they meant. Our response was what won the round for us. We said that while we did not specifically label links, brinks, and impacts in our disadvantages, and didn't even clearly understand what those debate terms meant, the essence of disadvantages in everyday decisions like where to eat or how to spend our money is this: cause and effect. We assessed causes and identified the effects of those causes. Since the causes of our opponents' case were clearly identified, all that was left was to demonstrate that the effects were a disadvantage. And that is what we had clearly done. Thus, the content of our argument was enough to make a real life decision and was also enough to make a decision in that debate round.

What Makes Debate Different From Real Life?

As a consequence of debate tournament format, one of the key differences from real life is that debate rounds allow you to test out certain positions for just an hour or so and see how they go in a practice environment. Debate rounds are testing grounds for logical weapons.

At the end of a board meeting, if you had persuaded the business to make a poor investment, you would have to face the consequences. In a debate round, if you persuade the judge to vote for your plan, we do not actually have to see if your plan was all that smart by facing the real life consequences. Do not mistake this to mean real wounds do not happen from debate—your words can hurt, your attitudes can make enemies, and your actions can have serious consequences. Yet you can walk into two debate rounds on the same topic and choose one argument in one round and a different one in the next round.

Another consequence of the debate format has to do with how your arguments are evaluated. Judges should only weigh the arguments of the other team against your arguments to make their decision (though they can offer their opinions as non-decision criticism on the ballot). In real life, your audience may think, "This is crazy!" and not be persuaded to act, even if nobody refuted your argument. In debate your arguments are supposed to be evaluated against the arguments of the other team by objective and mature judges, with the intent that judges provide criticism that helps you both to grow.

In the end, however, learning to accept criticism and when and how to abandon an initial position are valuable life lessons you will learn through debate. As a result, you need to discipline yourself to avoid practices that are not helpful in real life. Focus on gaining from debate those skills, abilities, and habits that will help you to make better decisions in life. Then debate will be an important, maturing tool in your life.

Debate Is Not Arguing, in the Argumentative Sense

Debate does not mean, "I will disagree with everything my opponents say." The point of debate is to learn to break down the rationale for a decision into pieces and evaluate those pieces. The best debaters will tell you they tend to agree with over half of what their opponents are saying (such as what is going on in the status quo, or even the main *point* of the case), while disagreeing only on certain key elements.

Let's say a team is arguing that baby trafficking (where babies are kidnapped and sold to Americans as "orphans") is a problem in the world, that the U.S. demand is the largest cause, and then they offer a plan to fix that problem. Should you argue "the babies are better off in America?" No! Don't say something patently ridiculous or inhuman just because you feel the need to disagree. Instead, agree, "This is such a terrible problem," and choose another argument! You can argue:

- The case does not fit within the topic (called a *topicality* argument).
- The plan doesn't do *enough* to solve the problem.
- This plan doesn't fix the problem, which will still remain after the plan.
- This particular plan causes disadvantages that outweigh its advantages.
- Here is a better plan.
- The status quo is already fixing the problem.
- There are alternate causes to the problem that are *embedded* in the plan.
- A higher international or Constitutional authority is needed, rather than the legislative (Congressional) authority used by the Affirmative.

There are all kinds of arguments you can make that even allow you to say, "babies being trafficked is terrible. This inadequate plan will not provide a solution to this problem. We must discard the AFF plan and look for a better solution." Debate is all about *choosing your battles*. Can you agree that this is an incredibly useful life skill?

An Isaiah story...

> In a debate round in high school my partner and I came up against a debate case that granted citizenship to a group of young people in the Northern Mariana Islands. These youth had been born during a decade that fell between two citizenship policies, leaving them without U.S. citizenship, even though their parents and younger siblings were citizens. Our opponents in this debate round spent all of their focus on the unfair situation of these stateless youth.
>
> So we agreed with 90% of their case. We agreed that the situation was unfair, and that it should be remedied. We disagreed with only 10% of what our opponents said. They proposed citizenship. We said that was not going far enough, that these youth should also receive compensation for a decade of lost opportunities. Our agreement with most of our opponents' case, especially their core idea, made our disagreement more compelling than if we had challenged every point. It was reasonable to agree, because the stateless youth truly had been wrongfully deprived of the benefits of citizens, such as in-state tuition at U.S. universities.
>
> We won the round because we agreed with what was reasonable, and our disagreement made sense, being more consistent with the affirmative team's perception of the unfair deal the "orphaned" citizens had received. I am fairly sure that our opponents even adapted their case as a result of our position in the round.

We have all found that the ability to agree with 90% of what people are saying in real life can work wonders. *Because* we agree on so much, the conclusion of those agreements is actually just something slightly different (our point of view) from what they are recommending (their point of view), because we are really arguing for the same thing in the end. It is just about how to achieve that end.

Agreement can diffuse many arguments and focus on really solving the problem.

> Agree with what you can, so you can disagree with what you must.

This principle holds true in real life as well as in competitive debate. Test every argument you make by the "real life" test, and you will find your debating makes more sense to you, to your opponents, and to your judges.

Chapter 2. What is Debate?

Five canons of Egyptian rhetoric

1. maintaining silence
2. restraining feelings
3. finding the right moment to speak
4. speaking fluently
5. speaking the truth

Observed by Michael V. Fox, "Ancient Egyptian Rhetoric", Rhetorica 1 (1983)

You probably think of debate as "speaking well" or "being articulate." To us, that just means delivering a speech. Delivery is only the most visible part of debate, but the majority of time spent by debaters is in the topic, while there are countless strategic decisions made during a round that the audience will never feel or notice. That's because debating well includes as much what not to say as what to say, and requires intense concentration while listening to someone whose job is to defeat your arguments. Being articulate will not cut it.

I always say that the best debaters, the truly national-class debaters, have a more thorough understanding of the basics than their intermediate competitors. And it's the secret to how I've seen countless novices leapfrog ahead: learning debate from a solid foundation skips years of beating around the bush. Unfortunately, too many coaches go for the shiny aspects of debate—the disadvantages, fallacies, counterplans, stock issues, and other terminology—skipping what debate is and does.

I have seen top-level nationals outrounds, determining who goes on to finals, determined not by the knowledge and presentation ability of speakers, but through their strategic ability. In these close rounds, the debaters who best understand and can explain what debate even is – at its most basic level – win these key rounds. They often win them by articulating these basics, and convincing the audience of what debate is – which is another way of answering the question: "why are we even here?"

Debate at its Core – A Definition

We define formal debate as: "Two sides disagreeing on a given topic for a given period of time, to an audience."

In mathematical terms: **Formal Debate = Topic + Sides + Format + Audience**

the parts of formal debate

This formula allows us to turn what could have been an informal discussion into a formal competition. Formal competition forces us to format our opinions and arguments in a way that encourages a rigorous examination of our topic. Debate provides a structure that actually lets us experience and understand what enables a hearty, yet productive exchange of ideas when we disagree with someone. If we let it, debate teaches us how disagreements should occur outside of the debate round as well.

Here's a basic overview of each term, though we've got a whole chapter on each coming up next.

- **Topic** – It's a *debateable thesis statement.* That means the topic is some claim, belief, or position that is falsifiable – there's a way to disprove it as much as a need to prove it.
- **Sides** – There are *assigned positions* on the topic. Debaters may not switch sides mid-round.
- **Format** – There are *time limits and a format of number of speeches and their order.* The format creates the strategy of the round, and can vary wildly. The best debaters are capable of owning their platform in a variety of formats, and use the format to their advantage. Lincoln-Douglas (1v1) and Cross-Examination (a 2v2 format) are common, but American parli, British parli, Crossfire/Ted Turner/Public Forum debates, Moot Court, Mock Trial, and many improvised formats exist, each with specific rules (like no new arguments after a certain stage, or switching speech orders, or more time for one party, or a rule that only a single argument may be provided in a final 1-minute speech).
- **Audience** – There is a *listening third party that will make a decision on the topic.* The debaters are not there to convince each other in formal debates; so an audience is not only necessary, but is actually the point of the debate. We want an audience to form an opinion based on the arguments presented, as they relate to the topic.

Roadmapping the Rest of Section 1

To learn a subject, it's best to break it into its parts, study these parts, practice, and then put the parts back together. So the next four chapters will proceed through each part of Formal Debate. Once you understand these parts, the book will progression through theories of persuasion, teaching you how to make a case, and conclude with some chapters on the tools of negative argument.

Chapter 3. Understanding
Types of Resolutions

The leader must aim high, see big, judge widely, thus setting himself
apart form the ordinary people who debate in narrow confines.
Charles de Gaulle

In formal debate, there is a narrow confine. Our job is to see through it – to find
the question behind the question. When debating privacy versus security, are
we not really asking ourselves: "what is the relationship of liberty and power?"
Debate starts with a topic. It doesn't end there, but a formal motion is needed to
begin the discussion, if a decision is to be had.

Usually we call the debate topic a *resolution*, *proposition*, or *motion*. It harkens
to parliamentary procedure, when a Congressperson proposes a resolution on
the floor of the House, or someone in a business meeting makes a motion. The
resolution, often simply called "the Rez," creates the debate.

Learn Parl procedure

Flavors of the Resolution

Debaters encounter three general types of resolutions. Debate leagues have historically and culturally parsed these resolutions in different ways, and all kinds of labels are given. The key is to classify and understand the *logic* of the statement to be proven, not to classify its name.

Each type of resolution will logically necessitate a different form of proof. Thus, to determine an approach to a topic, we must first determine what *type* of statement it is. Here we use the recently traditional names "policy," "value," and "fact" resolutions. If it were up to me, we'd stick with Classical Rhetoric and call them "deliberative" and "judicial" oratory, but sometimes you just have to go along with modernity.

Policy Topics

Policy resolutions identify a specific policy or policy area and state some sort of action that the team on the side of the resolution must support, whether vague or specific. Policy topics are questions of "deliberative discourse" in Classical Rhetoric. It's because determining what action to take, based on looking towards what potential futures are possible, is the stuff of business meetings, planning meetings, conventions, summits, and resolutions. These are the types of deliberations you will make your entire life, so learning policy debate really helps you learn effective habits of thinking for anytime you need to decide what to do.

A statement containing the following elements makes a policy resolution: An entity should act in a certain area.

In the following examples, see if you can identify the *entity,* versus <u>the action</u>, versus the **area of action**.

- The *U.S. Federal Government* should <u>significantly reform</u> its **agriculture policy.**
- The North Atlantic Treaty Organization (NATO) should significantly change its counter-terrorism policy.

- The U.S. should substantially reduce its dependence on foreign oil.
- The U.S. should withdraw troops from Afghanistan.
- The United Nations should sanction Syria.
- Google should start a cyber crime task force.

The common threads in all of these resolutions are the following elements:

- An "actor" (the U.S., NATO, etc.)
- An imperative word like "should"
- An action ("change," "withdraw," "start")
- A subject area ("agriculture policy," "dependence on foreign oil")

When the resolution merely states "change X policy," then there is no specified direction. When the team on the side of the resolution is free to take either direction under a resolution, the team defending the current situation/plan must prepare to defend the status quo in both directions.

Some resolutions, however, call for a specific direction, as in the Afghanistan example above. A team would not support the topic by arguing that "we should increase troops in Afghanistan," but only by arguing for a withdrawal of troops. However, if the topic had stated that the U.S. should "change its approach to the conflict in Afghanistan," then the team supporting the resolution could either withdraw *or* increase troops.

There is no rule on what makes a "policy resolution." Rather, a statement that demands some sort of action thereby also demands some sort of new policy. The *phrasing of the resolution* as an action makes the debate a **policy** debate—a debate about courses of action. And not everyone phrases their resolutions well, so you may end up with no actors, no areas, or even wonky actions to debate... your turn to be creative and reasonable in "interpreting" the resolution.

Policy resolutions are questions of action. *What should we do?* In policy debate we usually compare two courses of action: The proposed plan vs. the current plan (called the *status quo*)

> sta·tus quo (noun), *stātəs ˈkwō*
> the existing state of affairs, especially regarding social or political issues.
> "They have a vested interest in maintaining the status quo."
> Origin: Latin, literally 'the state in which.'
> *Oxford Dictionaries*

AFF will typically propose a specific course of action and show how it is better than the current plan. The other team usually shows that the proposed plan from AFF is not what we want to choose. Here's an example of a policy topic and a possible case.

Resolved: That the U.S. Federal Government should significantly change its policy toward Russia.

Today's World

The Status Quo (yes, right now!)—U.S. citizens can obtain Russian mail order brides.

- Russian women have a way out of a hard life.
- Russian women are able to find happiness in U.S. marriages, as in the many documented cases that exist.
- The U.S. Federal Government would not be taxed with the regulation of yet another unpreventable crime.

The New World

The Proposed Plan Big Idea—To outlaw mail order brides from Russia.

- U.S. citizens will not conduct trade with websites offering brides from Russia.
- Russian women are protected, not exploited and abused by U.S. citizens.
- Russian women are not treated as objects by U.S. citizens.
- Russian women are not coerced to leave their homeland and relatives.

Value Topics

Value resolutions are questions of principle. *How should we prioritize our values? What is the relationship between two "good" things, concepts, ideas, or philosophies?* Unlike in policy resolutions, whether the status quo is or is not effective is irrelevant. It's not a debate about what new action to take, so you could just as easily justify some existing policies as point to historical ones that worked well as point to some better future. Instead of competing plans, the debate focuses on that relationship between two goods, in situations where one must choose to prioritize one over the other.

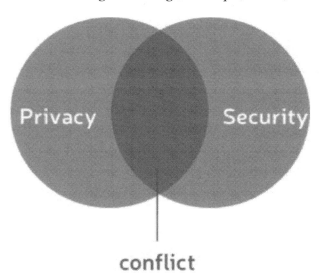

Value resolutions often identify a **specific value clash** between two values. It is not necessary that the values stated in the topic are directly contrary, but there must be *some* conceivable grey area where a choice is needed (note: NEG can certainly argue that no choice is ever needed). Thus, many value resolutions begin with the phrase "when in conflict," which means the debate is only about the values when they are in opposition. "Conflict" type clash is only one way to think of value debate. Hierarchy, frequency, social preference, and individual vs. collective need are other valid ways to debate a value resolution. Some value resolutions will identify a particular domain—including policy—and sometimes not. For example:

- When in conflict, cultural unity ought to be valued above cultural diversity.
- When forced to choose, a just government ought to prioritize universal human rights over its national interest.
- The security of society outweighs the freedom of individuals.
- When it comes to national leaders, results are more important than character.

Notice this key nuance: while it appears that AFF may have the "one side" and NEG "the other," in reality the entire phrase is part of the AFF's statement to prove. So don't fall into a trap of listing all the pros of cultural unity and cons of cultural diversity, without ever directly comparing the two to demonstrate how that makes the one preferable to the other. To do this, compare the best parts of cultural unity to the best parts of cultural diversity, or the worst of each, or both, but don't feel you've adequately proven the motion just focusing what ought be valued higher.

Value debate focuses on establishing a framework for choosing between the two goods. You'll do this through theoretical frameworks known as weighing mechanisms, and through examples and applications that illustrate your theoretical framework.

One massive pitfall to avoid: inside of many debate cases there is often a "value" that a debater will mention as "my value / our value / the value / you should value" or similar. This can be super confusing to all involved, because many will intuit that "value debate" refers to this value inside of a debater's case. That is not so. "Value debate" refers to the style of resolution – that there are two concepts to be evaluated against each other. The "value" that a debater puts into their case to assist in the evaluation of the values in the topic (yes... that's confusing) is not why this format is called "value debate." The values inside of cases appear in all types of debate, not just value debate. So watch for that ambiguity, because many debaters (and, unfortunately, many audiences) do not understand this distinction. It's a sad day when one debater agrees to the value in an opponent's case, and is perceived as losing the round. In reality, the debater is likely going to show that the opponent's value (in the case) supports the opposite value provided by the topic.

Fact Topics

Fact resolutions logically require evaluation of some concept, but do not require the concept to be directly compared to some other concept (as in value topics). *What should we think about X concept?* The first Fact Topic that I debated for a whole season was this: "WalMart's business practices are detrimental to the United States." (full case study at the end of this section)

Notice the evaluative aspect: we're going to determine whether the business practices of WalMart should be viewed as helpful, or detrimental. Fact debate doesn't mean you're debating true/false facts like the color of the sky or a math equation; fact debate means you're each evaluating some facts and arriving at different conclusions. The fact is proven through the debate round. So it's subjective: Subjective facts that logically require a perspective, worldview, or set of principles to evaluate.

Fact resolutions are phrased by joining a topic area with a subjective word or phrase. For example:

- Technology is killing our work ethic.
- Peace is undesirable.

- The Separation of Church and State is being inappropriately eroded.
- The media has lost its scruples.
- The Preemption Doctrine is unethical.
- Democracy is overvalued.

To debate a fact resolution is not that complex: describe the fact set to be evaluated, then use a framework of some kind to evaluate those facts. That's it. If that sounded complex, here's one word that sums it up: analysis. Fact debate is analyzing some issue. You do this all the time, and in all formats of debate. A fact resolution just narrows it down to a smaller chunk – no plan logically required, no named alternative to compare to, just analyze this discrete concept.

There are two primary areas of clash in fact debate:

> 1. **Debate over the nature of the fact set**: How much is the separation of church and state actually being eroded? What has the media done? What is the Preemption Doctrine? To what extent is democracy valued?

> 1. **Debate over how to evaluate the fact set**: Given the amount of separation of church and state, how should we think about it – appropriate, or inappropriate? Is this media activity beneficial? Is democracy's valuation proper?

By learning to show facts and activity in the status quo in policy debate, and by learning to prove one value greater than another in value debate, you will have the necessary skills for fact debate.

An Isaiah story...
A Fact resolution one semester in NEDA college debate read: "**Resolved:**

That Walmart's business practices are detrimental to the United States."

We had great statistics and figures on both sides of the topic. Let's look at a few cases that teams ran and the structure of the arguments we used in response to those cases.

A team from Bob Jones University ran a case that female employees of Walmart had been unfairly discriminated against by being paid less and not promoted when compared to men of equal experience, qualifications, and duration at Walmart. Thus, the two parts of the case were:

- Establish a value framework: Equal Treatment for Honest Work is the way to determine whether Walmart's business practices are detrimental.

- Establish the facts of the status quo: Walmart's women were treated unfairly.

We could challenge the framework, the facts, or both. In this particular case, we chose the following arguments.

- Agree to the value framework: Equal Treatment for Honest Work is a good lens through which to judge this round.

- Disagree with the facts: We argued that Walmart had amended its old practices and was currently treating women equally. Thus, their business practices "are" not detrimental to the U.S., in the present tense, and therefore the resolution has not been proven.

Obviously, a debate ensued. We actually debated this same argument-structure several times throughout the season. We won some and lost some. If you are thinking of other arguments to run—good! There was plenty to say and debating allows you to test different arguments.

Another time we debated a team from Duquesne University who challenged

Walmart's treatment of suppliers (the businesses that make the products Walmart sells). The two parts of their case were:

- Value Framework: Social Community is the highest value in determining whether Walmart's business practices are detrimental.
- status quo: Walmart is too harsh on suppliers and fractures social community by promoting an overly profit-centric mindset. Each person is part of the "machine" of the economy, encouraging sweatshop conditions.

We challenged both arguments of the case:

- Value Framework: Efficiency, rather than Social Community, is the way to judge Walmart's practices.
- status quo:

> First, the status quo does not violate my opponents' framework. Instead, Walmart promotes Social Community by providing cheap products that lower-income people can afford. Walmart is at the center of life for many people in America. This benefit outweighs harshness towards suppliers, and therefore shows that Walmart is not detrimental, even if you agree with my opponents' framework.
>
> Secondly, under the better framework of efficiency, Walmart blows our socks off. They invented the bar code, their shipping network is an industry standard, and they force suppliers to innovate to stay competitive. This is good for America.

We won some rounds using these arguments; we lost some using these arguments. The point is not our Win/Loss record, but that you can win or lose with perfectly good arguments from round to round. There are also other arguments you could make, but hopefully you see the two lines of argument most fact debates develop: the value framework and the status quo.

Summary: Types of Resolutions

Key Principle: Different topic phrasing demands different types of arguments.

Policy: x should be changed / x action should occur

- Examples:
    The U.S. should withdraw from Afghanistan in 2011.
    The U.S. Federal Government should significantly reform its criminal justice system.
- Key Points:
    There is a "status quo" which is current, and knowable.
    AFF must provide some action or plan that is *different from the status quo,* which they predict to lead to a better tomorrow.

Value: x is greater than y

- Examples:

In foreign policy, the U.S. should value moral principles over its own pragmatic interests.

When in conflict, cultural unity is preferable to cultural diversity.

- Key Points:

What the status quo is and defending it are irrelevant.

There is no "action" or change or plan.

A "value" is held as foremost by each team, in order to prove that its side of the resolution best achieves the value.

Fact:	x is [subjective term]

- Examples:

Walmart's business practices are detrimental to the United States.

Democracy is overrated.

- Key Points:

The team trying to support the resolution does not usually provide a plan.

The debate tends to center on what the status quo is, evaluating whether it is good or bad.

A weighing mechanism, just like in value debate, often becomes the centerpiece of the round.

The resolution should be a debatable statement that provides clear ground for two sides. Leagues try very hard to write resolutions where the ground, or strength of justifying arguments, on each side is fairly equal. Not everyone agrees on the names of these types of resolutions, so you'll have to learn the concepts and use your brain to adapt to the terminology.

Critical Takeaway

You use facts, values, and policies in evaluating every decision in daily life, just like in debate rounds. Facts, values, and policies are not arbitrarily separated in debate into cute, little boxes labeled "fact," "value," and "policy" debate. Debaters must marshal the available means of proof to support a resolution, which is usually phrased as a fact, value, or policy statement. In other words, you always have to think. There's no shortcut to thinking.

Just because we use the shorthand "value debate" does not mean that what I might say in value debate is not applicable in policy debate—it's just shorthand for "I'm debating a value topic." By understanding where the term "value debate" comes from (the resolution), you can understand *why* value debates are debated the way they are logically, not from any rule. You might utilize facts as you prove your side of a value resolution. You might use a value to justify your side of a policy resolution.

Debate is simply debate. You prove or disprove the resolution as is logically necessary, using whatever type of argument needed.

Chapter 4. The Roles of Each Side

Yer either fur it, or agin' it. Yew cain't have nuthin' betwixt.

The outcome of a formal debate round is much more all-or-nothing than an everyday discussion. The audience is literally forced to make a decision at the end of the round, and the debaters are literally forced to stick to their sides or risk "losing." It's my least favorite part about formal debate, because in real life it's essential to learn to make concessions, see the other side, admit when you're wrong, and follow when you thought you were going to lead. A debate partnership can teach you those things, but you typically won't learn much about them in an hour-long formal debate round. But still, keeping the sides assigned is pretty essential to the activity, so you're stuck with a side.

That doesn't mean you should disagree with yourself. Don't. You don't need to. The entire point of critical thinking is to take a large matter and break it into its parts, then analyze the parts. Even if you believe your opponent is doing generally the right thing, there are often objections you can make that are consistent with your view (e.g. "it doesn't go far enough," "it's imperfect and needs to be sent back to committee," "it's a great solution, in the wrong jurisdiction"). So don't view the assigned sides as distasteful, but rather as a challenge to get creative.

Sides Are Named

The affirming side will be called "Affirmative," "Proposition," or "Government." The negative side stands against the resolution (usually), and will be called "Negative" or "Opposition."

for	against
PROP	OPP
AFF	NEG
GOV	OPP
PRO	CON

common names for the sides

You will see these terms—AFF, GOV, PROP, OPP, NEG, PRO, CON—throughout the rest of the book. We are doing this because you would get rather of tired of reading the phrase "the team that affirms the resolution" every time we mention the AFF team. But please—don't say AFF and NEG or GOV and OPP in a debate round if your audience is new to the activity. Remember that your audience has probably not read this book (unfortunate for us both, for entirely different reasons).

You will need to say "the affirmative team" and so on when you are actually debating. Which is tough when you're switching sides five times in a day and accidentally refer to your own side with the opposite label. To keep it straight, we recommend always referring to the other side as "my opponents," so you don't have to remember that league's name for opponents.

Assigned Sides

In formal competitive debate, unlike real life, you will be on one side of a topic and cannot change without losing the round. It's not a rule; it's logical. If you stop disagreeing on the given topic, you stopped debating (by definition). And you can't win rounds if you aren't debating. In real life, you might change your mind in response to hearing an argument made by your friend. In debate, you have to stick to the side you were assigned for that round, 'til loss do thou parteth.

Function of Sides

The names are not as important as the function. The side you are assigned determines your position on the topic (resolution) for the entire round, as well as the type of strategy you will use to prove your points.

One side must "affirm" the resolution to win; the other side attempts to prevent that from happening. It's like offense and defense. Think of the AFF side as the side that "brought the motion forward" – AFF starts on offense. It's a key concept, because we will later teach you how many weak NEGs stay on defense, but the best find specific ways to go on offense.

It's just like in a normal conversation. Let's say you propose we go to the beach for vacation because it will be fun, we have the money, and it's a beautiful time of year for such a thing. A defensive and straightforward approach would be to say "nu-uh" to each of those three points for some reason or another. An offensive and more effective approach would be to say the big disadvantage is your boss will fire you from your job if you take another vacation so soon after the last one. This is "new material" that the defender brought out of thin air, putting the defender on offense because this seems to outweigh the other points. Now you are on defense in regards to this getting fired point. All that to say, great NEGs don't get trapped in their defensive roles; they find ways to go on offense.

Affirming the Resolution

The concept of affirming the resolution means to provide a case that proves the resolution "true."*

While that might sound like an overly simplistic approach, let's unpack the concept with an example resolution: "The United States should substantially reform its election system."

It is assumed that the statement is "not true" until AFF has proven otherwise, which they should do in the first speech by presenting a case. Obviously, the debate is about *whether* or not the U.S. should reform its election system, thus the resolution will teeter on "true" or "false" for the entire round. After the opening case is presented, the resolution should stand as "true," since no arguments have been given to the contrary.

Terminology note: It is the role of AFF to present a *prima facie* case for the resolution in the first speech of the debate round, or else there is nothing to negate. A case is not *prima facie* if, without negation from the NEG, the case does not support the resolution.

What is PRIMA FACIE?

Latin for: "At first sight; on the first appearance; on the face of it; so far as can be judged from the first disclosure ; presumably. A litigating party is said to

> have a prima facie case when the evidence in his favor is sufficiently strong for his opponent to be called on to answer it."
>
> *Black's Law Dictionary Free Online Legal Dictionary 2nd Ed. (thelawdictionary.org)*

Aesop's fable "Belling the Cat" includes a great idea to put a bell around the cat's neck, so that the mice will always know when the cat is coming. But the proposal includes no workable plan to actually get the bell on the cat's neck. In debate language, the presentation did not include a *prima facie* case. It's the basic burden of AFF to present a case that merits response.

Remember what I said about the best debaters knowing the basics of debate really well, and being able to talk about it to audiences? I often surprise debaters by arguing "their case is not *prima facie*" as one of my NEG strategies. It feels slightly insulting, but if there is good reason for it, audiences tend to see my side and many debaters struggle to articulate what about their case made it a *prima facie* case. This is particularly my favorite argument for value topics, when the AFF only points out the good side of one term of the resolution, without weighing it out against the good side of the other term in the resolution.

One of the key reasons you may argue a *prima facie* point is that you expect AFF to provide additional information in their second speech that takes the first speech's material and completes the case. This is no good because now the audience doesn't have the proper full testing of the AFF concept, starting from the first NEG speech. Instead, the first NEG speech may be wasted as AFF adapts (called "case-shifting") mid-round.

Is case shifting fair-play?

One final common *prima facie* argument is when AFF gives cross-examination responses to questions like "I have the full 79-page study that answers that, here I'll give it to you." Here we are concerned about whether the case could merit a vote for the resolution on its own, without the arguments and information NEG presents. Tricksy AFFs will try and waste NEG's time having NEG explain

AFF just to defeat AFF. NEGs are justifiably upset at being disadvantaged in that way, spending half their time being AFF too, and should resort to *prima facie* arguments as a recourse.

Why "true" is in quotation marks: Voting for winners is not really about truth in an absolute or philosophical sense. We say "true" or "false" because that's a convenient way to discuss a resolution. In a debate among students, however, the absolute best arguments for truth or falsity may never surface, or the issue itself may be so unknown that the "true" answer never even makes an appearance. Or perhaps the "truth" is so poorly defended that the inferior position wins. In debate, the scales tipping 51% towards one side or the other tends to create the decision for the judge, who must make a determination with the imperfect information presented within the time limits by the imperfect debaters. That mirrors real life, where one must often act on incomplete information, but also means we shouldn't assume that the side just proven "true" in a moment in time is therefore truth.

In debate rounds "affirming" the resolution means, **"the resolution seems more true than false, based solely on the arguments presented in the debate round today."** It makes enough sense to go ahead and use the words "true" and "false" without a doctoral dissertation on the meaning of truth.

After the Resolution Has First Been Affirmed

Let's assume AFF presented a case to implement national online voting for the President in order to affirm the resolution that "The United States should substantially reform its election system." Once a *prima facie* case has been presented, the resolution has been affirmed by default. The rest of the debate focuses on whether or not the resolution should continue to be affirmed. NEG will present arguments, like pointing out that the President is elected by the states and it is therefore both illegal and a threat to liberty for the U.S. to implement a *national* online voting system. This NEG argument negates the resolution.

That's the purpose of constructive speeches: to put out the original reasons for and against affirming the resolution. While one certainly compares arguments in constructive speeches, the entirety of rebuttals is devoted to weighing out the arguments begun in constructives. The final rebuttals from both speakers in our example will most likely weigh the pros and cons of efficiency (national online voting) and liberty (the negative argument), assuming AFF successfully proved the legality of their plan.

If, at the end of the round, the judge believes AFF's rationale is not overcome by NEG's objections, then the resolution is affirmed: the U.S. election system should be substantially reformed (based on the arguments heard today). Certainly there may be other relevant arguments or better ways to view the issue, but affirmation of the resolution is all about the arguments presented in the time limits of that particular debate. When compared against each other for strengths and weaknesses, do the arguments presented by the debaters end up tipping the scales of the resolution towards "true" or "false"?

When Samantha the salesperson tries to sell you some Nike Air Max shoes, she is resolved that: You should buy Nike Air Max shoes. Samantha will try to prove the resolution true—and gain a sale. In order to convince you to buy the Nikes (affirm the resolution), Samantha has to make a sufficient case (*prima facie)* for you to buy the Nikes.

Negating the Resolution

According to the Oxford Dictionary, to negate means to "nullify; make ineffective." To negate is stronger than to simply disagree. In formal logic it means to take a p to a minus p. In debate it means to displace the arguments the other team has put forth, to balance their argument to a net effect of zero or less, to show them as ineffective.

Negating means to show that all arguments in favor of the resolution (presented in the time limits of the debate) do not support its affirmation.

Yes, that sounds as confusing as a double negative. What it really means is doubly positive: either defeat the *exact* case provided by the AFF team, or defeat the *resolution as a whole.* Usually, you do a little bit of both. The way the resolution is phrased determines how you negate it.

For example:

1. **The 16th Amendment of the U.S. Constitution should be abolished.** This resolution is something that can be negated directly, but you should certainly also address AFF's specific arguments in favor of the resolution.

2. **The U.S. should change a policy it has.** This resolution is something that would be next to impossible to negate directly, without winning some sort of theoretical debate about how the other team possibly does not exist or that all actions are the result of fate. You will need to respond exclusively to the AFF arguments, showing how they either do not justify the resolution or do not even support it.

Aff: justify or support resolution

The first resolution above is narrow, and the second is broad. Most resolutions fall somewhere in between, like this one: **The United States federal government should substantially increase its transportation infrastructure investment in the United States.**

It would be hard to negate this entire resolution, since at least one example of a case where the U.S. needs to invest more in transportation infrastructure surely exists. Out-of-the-box thinking would be required to negate the whole resolution– for example, arguing that due to the national debt, the U.S. should freeze all of its spending, which would negate any increase in spending. But that would also be almost impossible to prove, since safety is a part of the transportation infrastructure, and AFF could outweigh the national debt argument with a policy that champions human safety.

NEG would have to negate whatever specific case AFF put forward in their effort to justify this resolution. But NEG could also cast doubt on the U.S. adding to the national debt, as a complimentary argument, especially if the AFF case is not linked to safety. For example, if AFF put forth a plan to pave old interstates with a new type of smooth asphalt that would reduce the amount of energy needed by vehicles, NEG would need to negate AFF's case by showing how this plan is a bad idea in some way. Perhaps the new asphalt has not been tested enough or there is evidence that it requires more maintenance. If NEG can negate AFF's case, NEG negates AFF's justification of the resolution. If NEG shows that AFF's case doesn't prove the resolution, and also shows that an increase in federal spending is not a good idea right now, then NEG has probably won the debate round.

What does "won" the debate mean? It means that based on the arguments provided in this round, and nothing more, the audience's most logical decision is to choose your position. That may be a "do this" position or a more negative "don't do it" sort of position. **Learning to be positive when you're negative is one of the most crucial lifelong skills available for mastery through debate.**

Summary

The affirmative team (AFF, GOV, or PROP) in the debate round will affirm, uphold, justify, or prove the resolution. The negative team will argue against the affirmative team's position, or against the resolution. When the teams are affirming and negating the same points—actually engaging each other's arguments instead of talking past each other—we call that engagement "clash."

Chapter 5. Owning the

Platform Across Formats

The format is the structure or form where the rules of a debate live. All the human-made rules live there (i.e., beyond the rules of logic, philosophy, rationality, and so on . . . which are debatable). Most formats will stick to obvious principles: roughly equal speaking time per side, providing interruptible and protected time for each speaker, and fair access to materials/evidence.

Multiple formats of debate allow you to cross-apply your skills. Each format serves a slightly different purpose and has advantages and disadvantages. For example, Parliamentary debate hones your ability to persuade using mostly common knowledge. Advantage: You can sharpen your ability to use logic in structuring your arguments without having to spend hours on research. Disadvantage: You might be tempted to use thin or trite arguments when you are given an unfamiliar resolution.

As another example, Team Policy Debate teaches you how to present a well-developed, well-researched case. Advantage: You learn how to rebuild your case over and over, since you generally stick with one case for an entire year.

Disadvantage: With so much focus on researched evidence, other forms of proof (logic, axioms, historical examples, analogies) can be completely overlooked.

It is valuable to learn many formats and to master specific ones. Let's look at the differences between prominent formats.

Key Format Items Vary by Debate Style and League

- Time Limits: Speakers who stray too far from the time limit, on either side, look like they lack confidence and might even be scored lower on speaker points for poor organization or rule violations.
- Speaker/Side Order: Does the first speaker also have the final rebuttal? Do some speakers have more speeches than others?
- Types of Time Blocks: Constructive speeches, cross-examinations, rebuttals, and preparation time.

Two Major Types of Speeches: Constructives and Rebuttals

Foundational arguments are put in place during the constructive speeches. These foundational arguments are then hashed out in the rebuttal speeches. New arguments are prohibited in the rebuttals, and therefore should be ignored, except to point out that your opponent has introduced a new argument in rebuttals. New evidence, additional analysis and more support should be presented in rebuttals to explore arguments already on the table to greater depth, but completely new lines of argumentation are forbidden.

The line between new support and new arguments is grey and debatable, but the principle is clear: good decisions are made after two sides have had ample time to hear and respond to each other's arguments. New rebuttal arguments do not provide clarity in decision-making, because there is not enough time left in the round to properly address the issue. When you bring an argument up in the first (constructive) speech and debate it for the following seven speeches, both sides have had time to evaluate it deeply, and the judge has heard enough to determine the best outcome.

In rebuttals, debaters should focus on developing refutation of known arguments, not try to cleverly outwit your opponent with a "gotcha" new argument.

- Interaction: Is there a cross-examination period? Are there points of information? Is there an open discussion period? Can you just ask the other team for a piece of paper they may have used? Can you pass your teammate a note mid-speech (tag-teaming)?
- Role of the Audience/Judge: Some formats allow audible support from the audience, while others may have a moderator or even reality TV style critique mid-round. In parliamentary debate, the judge must rule on points of order, but may need your help knowing how. In moot court, judges cross-examine you for nearly ten minutes within the round.

A core point of this book is to help the speaker acquire self-sight—the ability to objectively see yourself in third person, from an audience's perspective. Knowing how to use your format is a key to self-sight. Here are two principles to consider:

1. Great Speakers Own Their Format

At first glance, format seems unimportant. Not so. In *Confessions of a Public Speaker*, Scott Berkun devotes almost an entire chapter to simply managing your room—complete with a scathing review of conference-room chandeliers. Tomes have been written on how to manage your time at the podium. Ethos even runs a series called Own Your Platform, devoted to format issues for businesspeople.

The best debaters are not only masters of their content and public speaking, but masters of the format. In life, it means comfortably knowing and utilizing the rules, customs, and exceptions to a meeting, assembly, or conversation, not only so that you know how to navigate the situation, but so you also know how to properly respond to an opponent who makes a procedural misstep.

When you own your format, you are willing to take the big risks that inspires the audience—like a professional singer who learns to move and dance in a live performance, a flight attendant who tells jokes, or the customer service representative who sincerely apologizes.

2. Format Can Save You, But Using It Has Risks

Knowing the format is like using The Force: there is a light side and a dark side.

Most debaters are totally passive when exceptions to the format occur. Here are a couple of extreme stories where the format was utilized effectively. In reality, most encounters about debate format involve the exchange of printed materials with an opponent, correction of a mistaken time when someone forgets speech lengths, or telling the judge how many speeches are left in the round.

All format interactions that do not simply let the flow of the debate happen to you bring inherent risk, but so does letting the debate just happen. Once I let my opponent give an 8-minute rebuttal, when only 5 minutes were allotted, because I did not know what to say. The judge never even knew. Interrupting the speaker to enforce the time limit could have cast a negative light on me; allowing my opponent to have 3 extra minutes of speaking time could have tipped the debate to my opponent's side. To interrupt or not to interrupt—both are risky.

Three Stories

Format schmormat. Could you give us some examples? Yes.

Story 1: Interrupting Self

An Isaiah Story...

Once in a parliamentary debate round, a format where the speaker may be interrupted by the opposing team for points-of-information, I needed my opponents to accept one approach, and not another. I could either set up a catch-22 with many words, or get the other team to commit to the most favorable choice mid-speech, cutting my burden of argumentation in half. Parliamentary rules do not state whether or not a speaker may ask for a response from the other team. Typically, the speaker receives, rather than asks, the point-of-information questions. Yet I simply asked my opponents the question: "Will you drop topicality if we admit to this portion of our plan, meaning your disadvantage is clearly caused by our plan?" They were surprised, said "yes," and allowed me to outweigh their disadvantage (difficult!) without wasting two minutes defending topicality.

Some may view my unusual tactic as inappropriate. It led to a better discussion of ideas; however, it required me to take a risk. Not every risk is "inappropriate"—it's simply a risk. A judge who felt the move was inappropriate could have deducted points from me. I took stock of my audience and opponents, had a solid understanding of the rules, and deemed it a worthwhile course to pursue. Yes, debaters exercise judgment constantly. Everyone agreed at the end of the round that the judgment had been good, and my team won.

Certainly an audience may be turned off by the use of format. For example, a participant in a meeting might speak for 20 minutes if time limits were

> not set. But the audience may then be annoyed or bored by the speaker. Not every course of action is wise.

Story 2: Speech Time as Prep Time

> *An Isaiah Story...*
>
> Have you ever given a terribly disorganized speech when you felt that just one more minute of prep time would have made the difference? The problem was not with your idea. The problem was just organizing your ideas and making sure you had the flow right. Well here is a format hack that I've used a few times, which many of my debaters have also used: take the first minute of speech time as prep.
>
> Does this sound risky? It is risky and makes you look ill prepared. Yet if you are going to deliver a mind-blowing speech because of the prep, then take the risk!
>
> In another case, the other speakers ended their speeches five minutes early to try and throw off my team. With no prep time between speeches (it was parliamentary debate), I was nowhere near prepared yet to attack their idea. I've learned since then to prepare responses *as* they are speaking, but in this case I figured I should take some of my speech time to prep. In the end, my speech was longer than theirs, far better than it would have been had I not taken the risk, and we won.
>
> Do not use this tactic as a crutch! If you are a novice, I promise you, you do not need this tactic. You need to push yourself to be capable of filling all your speech time before you start making exceptions.

Story 3: Unusual Prep

> *An Isaiah Story...*

For one tournament in college I partnered with Travis Jordan, a fantastic debater with another innovation I will share with you later, called the "anti-value." I had never seen Travis debate before this college tournament. He had a habit of ending "idea" prep-time in our team value and team policy rounds by standing up from the prep table and going to the lectern. But he would tell the judge that he was not yet finished with prep time! That seemed strange and outside of normal debate customs, but there's no reason it was not legal. I asked him why he did that. He said it helped him organize the speech with crystal clarity and it ensured the best moments were prepared by rapidly running through the speech in his head from the lectern, rather than from the table. He could also fill in any notes or key lines that were missing. I ended up copying the habit regularly! You should burn only 20-40 seconds this way, but it shows you are going the extra mile to prepare more than your ideas alone, and almost always pays off.

No debate round, meeting, or assembly goes exactly according to the plan you have in your mind. Thus, learn to manage your format as one of the ways to adjust. Numerous formats of debate exist, some that are even formed for a single, specific event. To be sure, each format lends itself to its own key strategies. At the end of the day, however, you will use the available facts to make arguments to support a position in a communicative way, no matter which format you debate.

If you are effective at format management, you will likely be an effective teacher and meeting presenter, if not event organizer.

Common Debate Formats

Here's a crash course in typical debate formats.

Cross Examination Debate

CX debate, commonly referred to as "team policy" or TP debate, begins with two teams of two individuals squaring off as AFF and NEG. Team value debate occasionally uses this format, but in the top three high school leagues, it is TP that uses the CX debate format. So most people mean CX when saying TP.

- Rounds begin with four constructive speeches, lasting 8 minutes each.
- Each constructive is followed by 3 minutes of CX, where someone from the other team asks questions of the previous speaker.
- Rounds end with four rebuttals lasting 5 minutes each.

Speakers:

- 1A = 1st Affirmative speaker
- 2A = 2nd Affirmative speaker
- 1N = 1st Negative speaker
- 2N = 2nd Negative speaker

Speech names:

- 1AC = 1st Affirmative Constructive Speech – 8 min.
    Cross-Ex by 2N – 3 min.
- 1NC = 1st Negative Constructive Speech – 8 min.
    Cross-Ex by 1A – 3 min.
- 2AC = 2nd Negative Constructive Speech – 8 min.
    Cross-Ex by 1N – 3 min.
- 2NC = 2nd Negative Constructive Speech – 8 min.
    Cross-Ex by 2A – 3 min.
- 1NR = 1st Negative Rebuttal Speech – 5 min.

- 1AR = 1st Affirmative Rebuttal Speech – 5 min.
- 2NR = 2nd Negative Rebuttal Speech – 5 min.
- 2AR = 2nd Affirmative Rebuttal Speech – 5 min.

Each person gives a constructive speech and a rebuttal, and conducts a CX.

So for example, the 1A (first affirmative speaker) will give the 1AC (first constructive speech), will CX the 1NC (first negative constructive speech), and will give the 1AR (first affirmative rebuttal).

Negative Block: You will notice that the 2NC and 1NR are back-to-back negative speeches. These two speeches are referred to as the "negative block," because the negative gets 13 minutes of speech time when added together. AFF usually gets the last word in debate, since AFF has the burden of proof to support the resolution—a more difficult challenge (from a purely logical standpoint, not necessarily in specific rounds). The advantage of two consecutive speeches in the negative block helps balance out the advantage of the affirmative's last word.

Prep Time: Each team is usually allotted five minutes of prep time in this format. Most leagues only allow the use of prep time before speeches, though some allow use of prep time before CX or don't have a rule on the subject.

? Does stoa have a rule on prep time CX

Lincoln-Douglas Debate (LD)

LD means "one-on-one" in debate lingo, named Lincoln-Douglas after the famous Presidential debates between Abraham Lincoln and Frederick Douglas.

You do not have a partner in LD debate. Speech times vary, but the following is a common format:

Speech Times:

- AC = Affirmative Constructive Speech – 6 min.

    Cross-Ex – 3 min.
- NC = Negative Constructive Speech – 7 min.

    Cross-Ex – 3 min.
- 1AR = 1st Affirmative Rebuttal Speech – 4 min.
- NR = Negative Rebuttal Speech – 6 min.
- 2AR = 2nd Affirmative Rebuttal Speech – 3 min.

Prep Time: 3 minutes each

AFF has one constructive and two rebuttals; NEG only has one constructive speech and one rebuttal speech. Again, this format gives AFF the last word. Each side is usually allotted 3 minutes of prep time in LD.

American Parliamentary

Modeled after British parliament, the resolution changes each round, rather than each month or each year, in Parli-style debates. Don't ask why; we don't know—it's great fun though. Parli has no CX, but does have Points of Order, Points of Information, and other interruptions of a speaker's normal speaking time. The speaker "has the floor" while speaking and can choose to recognize certain points, while other points stop the timer and require a ruling from the judge.

The "Government" (GOV) and the "Opposition" (OPP) correspond to the AFF and NEG in other debate formats. The Prime Minister leads the Government, and his partner is the Member of Government. That's because in parliamentary systems, "the Government" is the party that proposes policies, and is led by the Prime Minister. The Leader of Opposition and Member of the Opposition form "Her

Majesty's Loyal Opposition." Here is one common American Parli structure – just know that times often vary between leagues.

Speakers:

- PM = Prime Minster
- MG = Member of Government
- LO = Leader of Opposition
- MO = Member of Opposition

Speeches:

- PMC = Prime Minister Constructive – 7 min.
- LOC = Leader of Opposition Constructive – 7 min.
- MG = Member of Government (Constructive) – 7 min.
- MO = Member of Opposition (Constructive) – 7 min.
- LOR = Leader of Opposition Rebuttal – 5 min.
- PMR = Prime Minister Rebuttal – 5 min.

Points of Information: other participants may request for a moment of the speaker's time to make a point of information ("POI"). It is up to the speaker to decide how many points to grant and when, to whom.

Prep Time: 15 minutes before the round, but zero inside of the round

As you can see, the negative block (MO and LOR) allows GOV to have the last word. The MG and MO speeches do not contain the letters R or C, since the member speakers give only one speech per round, but these speeches are considered "constructive" speeches where new arguments can be made.

One special rule: the first and last minutes of any speech are "protected time," where points of information are out of order.

British Parliament (BP)

A style of debate that tends to judge more of the skills of individual speakers, British Parli has a plethora of formats, though it usually includes more than two teams. In the American collegiate version of BP, four teams of two will debate. You will have an "upper house" (the first four speakers) and the "lower house," with GOV and OPP designations. Judges rank the teams from 1-4, and the better teams rack up more points. So at the end of the round, the audience is not voting for the topic, but for the teams – so you often have one GOV and one OPP team getting the top two slots.

Speech times vary, though 7 minutes for each speaker is pretty common. BP places slightly less emphasis on refutation and greater emphasis on persuasion and overall communication. You set yourself apart from the others on your side by having more clever arguments that carry the round forward in a powerful way. By ranking the teams in order of skill, rather than voting for or against the resolution, judges emphasize individual communication more than the connection between the arguments and the resolution.

The Key to Formats

Use your format to your advantage. For example, asking for some quotation from the other team is a common request in team policy (and other formats, occasionally). Many debaters waste some of their CX time with this administrivia. Debaters who own their format ask for such info as soon as CX is over. As you become a master of your format, you'll start to see what's happening on stage *through your audience's eyes*. And that will give you comfort to be relaxed, conversational, and occasionally funny, as you loosen up from just presenting facts and information and instead start creating an entertaining or moving debate.

? Need more explanation

Chapter 6. Connecting with the Audience

Muhammad Yunus (photo by Jmquez)

Mohammed Yunis visited the United States as a 15-year-old Boy Scout from Bangladesh. He returned 57 years later to receive the Congressional Gold Medal as a social entrepreneur who is changing the mindset that business is about the bottom line (money) to a more human perspective—that business is about problem-solving. Yunis received the Nobel Peace Prize in 2006 for founding the Grameen Bank, one of the most famous microfinance initiatives (and something I've encountered as an example in many debate rounds). True to the Boy Scout model of leadership, he ranks empathy as the key to making human connections, and therefore of being a "changemaker." Yunis belongs to Ashoka, an international foundation with a goal to teach school children empathy, in addition to math and reading.

When I was in leadership training Eagle Scout in the Boy Scouts of America, empathy was listed as the first quality of a good leader. That really stood out to me, because people often think of leaders as people who know what to do and tell others what to do, but empathy means seeing through the eyes of others.

> Empathy: "the action of understanding, being aware of, being sensitive to, and **vicariously experiencing** the feelings, thoughts, and experience of another of either the past or present without having the feelings, thoughts, and experience fully communicated in an objectively explicit manner"
> *Merriam Webster*

Empathy allows you to put yourself in someone else's shoes. If you are going to change the world, or even just change one person's mind in a debate round, you need to perceive what you are saying through another person's mindset.

Effective communication does not take place simply with a clearly stated message; effective communication takes place when the message is clearly understood.

Communication 101 college classes begin with the idea that communication has to include both the sender and the receiver of the message.

Oddly enough, in a formal debate round you are not trying to convince your opponent. Your opponent did not choose his side, but he has to stick with it throughout the round. You are trying to convince the audience. Presidential debates in the United States operate in a similar way. For example, in the debates held prior to the U.S. presidential election of 2012, Obama did not really think he would change Romney's mind. Obama was trying to change the audience's mind.

In formal debate, the audience is usually called a judge or a critic. You may have one judge, or a panel of judges that you are trying to win over to your side. The judge is the one weighing the arguments on both sides of the debate. He/she will cast a vote for one side or the other at the end of the debate round. Other people may or may not be in the room during your debate round, but your connection should be primarily with the judge.

So let's talk about how to approach an audience, loving them enough to see through their eyes. This concept is the major part of what Aristotle meant by "Pathos," the idea of putting your audience in the right frame of mind to hear your message. Besides credibility (Ethos) and your argument (Logos), Pathos is the third form of artistic proof that Aristotle observes in *Rhetoric*.

Forming a Connection

Photographer Richard Renaldi created a photographic project in 2007 called *Touching Strangers,* in which he had complete strangers create spontaneous relationships by filming three people together who did not know each other previously. Renaldi had the strangers pose with each other *as though* they knew each other. The subjects found that they could make connections with strangers, and even enjoyed it!

Your judge (audience) may be a total stranger to you, but because he/she is human, you share many similarities. You probably both prefer a lively, interesting debate round over a dull one. You probably both care about truth. You probably both truly want the world's problems to be solved. And here's an encouraging thought: you probably both want you to speak well. That's right. Audiences want speakers to do well. Audiences empathize with how difficult it is to stand up and defend your ideas, and probably admire you greatly!

So breathe deeply, look your judge in the eyes, know that your judge wants you to do well, and form a connection with your judge. Sometimes you have a chance to ask questions before a round begins, but notice from the definition of empathy, that whatever it is cannot be fully described in words from someone else. Seeing through someone's eyes is deeper than that.

Three Communication Languages

Part of understanding your audience in order to connect with them means understanding that different people process information differently.

Visual	Kinesthetic	Auditory
Picture	Gestures	Listening
Drawings	Touching	Sounds Patterns
Shape	Body Movements	Rhythms
Sculpture	Object Manipulation	Tone
Paintings	Positioning	Chants

Visual learners "see" things in their minds. When you speak, a visual learner will form mental pictures. A visual learner will communicate understanding by saying: "Oh, I see what you mean."

Auditory learners process information through sound. Your volume, tone, rhythm and pace contribute to their listening process. When auditory learners agree with you, they might say, "that sounds right."

Kinesthetic learners learn more spatially. They respond to a speaker who communicates through movement and gestures. A kinesthetic learner might say, "I **feel** that this policy should be adopted, and we should **throw out** the old approach."

Most people favor one mode of processing information, but also process in the other modes to some degree. Since you will not know how your judge learns, and since most people learn in some combination of the modes, you should be sure to speak in a full-orbed way—painting mental images (e.g., through story-telling), varying your volume, tone, rhythm, and pace in ways that express the meaning of your content, and using meaningful gestures and body movement to connect with your judge.

Consider the difference between:

- *Abstract Statement:* Our policy should be adopted because it has the most benefit to society. The advantages outweigh the disadvantages. For all these reasons, please vote for me.
- *Optimized Statement:* What we've got today, it smells fishy. I hope you can see the vision here: our policy's healthiness is worth the pain of growing new muscles. Faster, better, cheaper? It's worth voting for.

Many communicators are frustrated with audiences who don't seem to respond, because "I said the right words" – but that doesn't mean that you got through. Don't forget that debating is a human experience. The judge is not a vending machine where you can put in the right arguments and get a winning ballot in return, but a human being who has to process your arguments in order to understand them.

Your audience will consider what he/she *understands*.

What debaters say ≠ What judges understand

So stay in tune to your audience so that you can gauge his/her understanding. This self-awareness is tough to cultivate, but you must push yourself to do it. I've been in far too many business meetings with self-absorbed CEOs saying words, words, words, or sales people presenting their pitch, or entrepreneurs asking for money, and you'd be amazed at how clear it is that they only are thinking about themselves. People tune out, are skeptical, don't understand – the effective speaker first and foremost anticipates this and prevents it, but secondly can recognize and adapt in real time.

If your audience starts nodding off, tell a lively story. If your audience has glazed-over eyes, change the pace or step away from the lectern. If your audience looks confused, quit using "debate" language, use an example, explain where the idea came from, and say "you're probably thinking…". If your judge falls asleep, cry – you probably waited too late to read the signs of the times.

Avoid Pandering

In emphasizing the connection you want to establish with your judge, let's also issue a warning: avoid pandering.

Why? Pandering is a bad substitute for good support at best, and at worst, it is offensive to your audience.

You may have heard the ancient proverb "Beware of flattery." Flattery is one type of pandering. You say: "What a gorgeous necktie!" You mean: "I hope I just made you feel good, and that your good feeling will make you like my weak argument." Exaggerated deference is another form of pandering. You say: "Oh thank you that someone of your stature should grace the likes of lowly college debaters with your presence." But you mean: "I hope if I make you feel important enough that you will vote for me whether my opponents position is better than mine or not."

The content of what you say should never be displaced by improper attention to your audience.

Information designer and national speaker who packs out massive assembly halls, Edward Tufte, concludes his advice on speaking this way: "Know your content; respect your audience." Tufte's perspective reminds us to maintain the focus of a debate round on craftily communicating credible content. Relate to your audience respectfully, but do not cater to them. Former debater Amy Rutledge (now Amy McPeak) once quoted the Pope in a round where the judge was a nun, but it was appropriate because the quote supported Amy's point on free trade, and Amy was making a connection with her audience with legitimate content. If, however, Amy had gone on to talk about how much she loved the Pope, she would have been pandering – rather than focusing on good support for her position.

Appropriate connection versus inappropriate connection with your audience is a wisdom issue, meaning you will learn it over time and in various situations. Rules can get you started, but true wisdom comes from experience and a good, teachable heart.

How to Get Better

I often assign debaters to present their prepared case (e.g. 1AC) to a neighbor, then ask the neighbor:

- What did you hear?
- What do you think I'm recommending?
- What was my best and worst example?

Most debaters are shocked by how little was retained. But that is a needed shock. Poor listeners then argue with their audience to try and inform them as to why they should've seen it differently. Great communicators accept that what someone heard is what they heard, and the communicator can and must improve to be heard better, and has a WIDE variety of tools to do so: pitch, tone, pace, eye contact, physical movement, figures of speech, rhythm, imagery, quotes, stories, examples, pauses, volume, simplifying content, and rhetorical questions.

Don't let the "they didn't seem to hear a word that I said" shock happen to you.

10 Ways to Get Your Audience to Want More

I originally wrote this advice for business-people, but have slightly repurposed it for debate. Here are 10 things you can do to create a "we want more from you" feeling rather than a "please make it stop" feeling.

1) **Know Why You're There.** And then stop once you're done with that. This is the hardest discipline of a speaker and necessitates iterations of outline to analysis to speaking to outline to analysis. Every time you express your idea, you find greater clarity on its essence. If you cannot say why you are there with a simple sentence, you don't deserve to be there yet and have more thinking to do. Don't put the job of processing primarily on the audience. They are busy enough understanding and creating analogies to their own life.

2) **"Respect your audience, know your content."** That's what brilliant information visualization guru Edward Tufte says to choose instead of over-analyzing the audience. It's seeing from your audience's perspectives as humans, not a special class of people who don't know something. Don't mind read. That's patronizing. People remember the speaker that treated them as intelligent, and simply not informed yet on that particular issue. Being more informed on one issue acknowledges that anyone in the audience could change roles with you if the topic were different; you're not "better than them" and they know you don't think you are.

3) **Believe what you're saying.** Like John Kerry (a former Presidential candidate) doesn't. It's all in the eyes. Charisma is possible for everyone that makes a value commitment to the information presented. If you can't, you

probably don't have a point... Which means you shouldn't be there, and shouldn't be asked back, and probably made an excuse People love to hear again from someone like Simon Sinek who really believes in the importance of their message, because a little of that spark will rub off.

4) **Know what persuasion means and doesn't.** Nobody "wins" as you facilitate an observation of what should take them from thinking A to thinking B – the practical definition of persuasion. Audiences come back to the speakers that work from shared assumptions, add great facts, and lead to an unexpected conclusion. They do not appreciate the same way a speaker who acts like both facts and good decisions on those facts are a possession of the speaker. As you learn along with the audience, all of you third parties in admiration of the information conveyed, the persuader becomes the planetarium director. The stars, not the speaker, are the point... And you've removed yourself enough to be invited back.

5) **Help the audience enjoy the memory**. Likeable people are recommended. Self-depricating humor, jokes and stories, tying in current events, all while being relevant. No cheese. This isn't carte blanche for your lawyer jokes or latest news clippings or attempts to be relevant with YouTube hits. Go for... actual relevance. Most people remember no presentations a month later, because they didn't enjoy it enough to want a memory.

6) **Move it along**. In many contexts, just keeping the momentum moderately upbeat will accomplish point 5. In any case, those who do speak moderately fast are perceived as more intelligent, and have the ability to end sooner than expected. Usually a yay. The mistake is to speak quickly under some sort of pressure. Speaking pressured is never good, because it rubs off and makes an audience impatient. It's the relaxed, confident, quick, but still ending early speech that people love. For competitive debaters, it's the relaxed person that isn't talking past the beep, but is able to end just before. You don't need more words to get through.

7) **Do some single abnormal thing**. Abnormal for what is expected of the type of speech you're giving. Take a risk.

Interact with the audience and manage the room like a teacher. It's always a risk, but well worth it. Involve your audience in the PROCESS of discovering and owning the truth you're presenting.

- Wear something strange and quirky. I once went to a security briefing by a spy who had a polka dot suit on under his trench coat to demonstrate a point. It's memorable, where I cannot remember how many speeches I've forgotten ?
- Use a running metaphor. A student struggling with a persuasive on why you shouldn't buy from Starbucks (that's not the point here...) took her speech to the next level when she added a running metaphor about friendly-fire for important causes.
- Have the audience stand up and do some stretches half way through.
- Turn off the lights and speak in complete darkness about a truth you will reveal.
- Write and deliver a haiku or spoken word poetry with feeling.

Those are all for business communicators. Debaters cannot do most of those things, but should find analogies:

- Pause for a full 15 seconds to let something sink in
- Build epistrophes, anaphoras, or even a haiku, to build the emotion or simplify the essence of your argument
- Spend 2-3 minutes laying the foundation for a moving, inspiring, or hilarious story that proves the entire point

8) **Be humble.** Let what you're saying speak for itself, not your spin on it. And don't be "too perfect." Sometimes a simple rearrangement can do the trick. Don't start with what your company does, but with a problem everyone has. Two

weeks ago I coached a CEO presenting to an audience of CEOs and we switched even the "hi my name is and I do" part until later in the presentation after the "CEOs like you usually face one of the following three roadblocks in marketing." This put the audience, not the presenter, first.

9) **Share a watercooler-worthy nugget that goes viral**. Something they can repeat to their friends that probably nobody has ever heard. So not the 10,000 hours from Gladwell's Outliers, which is interesting but not fresh. But it's LIKE the 10,000 hours. Concrete, repeatable, and new. In debate, most audiences go back to the judge room and tell others about their rounds. You want to be the speaker that becomes the talking point because you shared some new example, or surprising factoid about something the audience thought they knew.

10) **End on a high note**. People will say "that was awesome!" if the last impression was.

The good news is that you can do this! It doesn't take genius, just discipline. Discipline to what? Be simpler, stick to the point, avoid speculation too much, enjoy yourself and let the audience do it too, and refuse to let yourself on the stage until there is something interesting to share.

Be what you wish for when you're in the audience, and audiences will want you back.

Chapter 7. Primary Tool:

"The Flow"

If debating is all about convincing an audience, then how do you keep track of what the audience hears, the way the audience hears it? And how do you plan what you're going to say next?

If you do not learn to take good notes, you will lose track of arguments after 30 minutes or an hour. You'll use a legal pad and small handwriting for this activity, which helps you see how arguments flow from start to finish.

In formal debate, we call this note taking "flowing." That's because you're keeping track of how an argument develops – keeping the flow of an argument organized. So your legal pad is actually a flowpad, you trade flows from previous rounds, you analyze the flow from a past round, your flowing is always in multiple colors, and you draw doodles on your flowsheet when you have to pretend your listening but can't seem to pay attention.

Flowing is more than your listening and argument tracking device. You prepare your next speech in the same way you take notes, on the same paper, right next to the other arguments. You'll speak from an outline in debate speeches, and your flow keeps what you're going to say organized.

You likely will use little colored stickies or something to help you remember when you intended to quote an outside source, which you label with the same colored sticky in your binder. Sound complicated? It's not too challenging, and you'll learn quite a bit about organization.

Equipment: You can get ripped off buying large paper in a spiral binding from folks, or make your own, as you start to develop flowing preferences. I prefer legal-sized loose white printer paper myself these days, but used to prefer white legal-size legal pads. I've known debaters who get jumbo art pads, or use specifically colored paper for specific things. Perhaps it's helpful, but I think at that point it's more like obsessing over the color of your socks—makes you feel good to do it, but isn't terribly important.

An Isaiah story...

At one Ethos Debate Camp we had a debater that we still affectionately remember as "no flow boy." He was convinced that he was a polymath (he probably was and is, actually), and because of that he adamantly insisted that he flowed in his head. In two practice debate rounds there, he certainly executed effective speaking, was highly persuasive, and was incredibly organized, but he did not directly refute or accurately summarize the points from his opponents.

He was a fourth-year debater, and complained that he should be at the highest level of nationals but the judges are so ridiculous that he often loses rounds he should win. What was clear to everyone but him, was that he was not listening well, and therefore not engaging directly in what others were saying (even if they were less "smart"). As coaches, every single one of us lasered in on not flowing as the root issue, but he refused to do it.

The thing is, he was a genius. He really was. He knew everything about everything – it was stunning. But debating isn't a one-way speech activity. It involves a great deal of listening and responding. So genius alone doesn't cut it. Debaters must learn to listen well.

> And thus, someone with potential as a top 10 nationals competitor never even qualified to nationals. No flow boy hit the flowing ceiling.

The most common problem I find with intermediate debaters who are frustrated that they are not going to the next level of debate is simply that they are not flowing properly. Learning to take notes is that important.

In fact, I have never known a debater to be successful at high levels of debate (regional and national championships) who is unable to flow. Eventually, every successful debater learns to flow.

If you resist learning to flow effectively, you effectively limit how well you can do in debate. Think of your note-taking ability as a "ceiling" for how high you can go. Debaters who cannot think as well, but do keep track of all the arguments, consistently perform better than those who are brilliant, but do not organize their ideas and the ideas of the debate round on paper.

Some people hear me say this and assume I am saying to debate like a dry, non-passionate policy analyst, going down their notes one by one. I am saying nothing of the kind! The flow is a great way to organize what is happening in the round, but not an excuse to throw out the communications techniques that make people want to listen to you. The flow is just one of many tools needed to succeed in debate – it's the one that helps you remember what others said and how they said it.

How to Flow: Popular Methods

After all that talk about the importance of flowing, you probably expect to hear "the way" to flow next. Thankfully, there are many ways to accomplish the two core goals of flowing:

1. Keeping track of what the audience heard, and

2. Arranging what you're going to say next

You probably will develop your own personal system for flowing. It's best to start like others do, and then work from there.

Take notes on all the arguments in a way that you can see the support and claims being made by each team on each argument throughout the round. Thus, you see the "flow" of an argument. You can accomplish this objective in a system that works for you, but we suggest starting out the same way 95% of debaters do. Divide your paper into columns for each speech in a round and track the arguments in those columns from left to right, writing responses next to the original claims.

As the example below demonstrates, debaters pick and choose certain arguments and even bring up new arguments that are not direct responses. Leave enough "white space" to make sure you can track arguments as they expand throughout the round. Here is a flow for a round on the resolution "The U.S. should withdraw from Libya," intended for a policy debate.

I. Definitions				
"Interventionism"				
– Using military force when no threat exists				
II. Libya Attacks				
– Launched X missiles	We Agree to these facts			
– Spent X $$				
– No Congressional authority				
III. Harms				
A. Immoral War				
B. Will Cause Radicalism	A. Not Immoral	A. Yes	Etc…	Etc…	Etc…
	1. Justified against Evil	1. Just War Theory contradicts – no authority		
	2. Fair Warning			
IV. Plan	B. Is creating friends	2. But no authority		
– Immediately cease military ops in Libya		B. No support!		
U. Solvency				
A. Ends Immoral War				
B. Prevents Radicalization	A. See Harms. It isn't			
		Argument		

What You're Looking For

1st – What the Audience Heard

Keep track of what the audience actually heard, not what it should have heard. That means the way things are presented, the emphasis, the credibility of the speaker at the time, noises in the room, and so on, affect what is heard and you have to constantly analyze what is most important. Two different debaters can say the exact same words in completely different ways – so reduction to words on your flowsheet alone will not represent what the audience heard.

2nd – Claims and Warrants: Theirs and Yours

The details of the support your opponents provide (warrants) are more important than the claim they are supporting. For example, if I said "the economy is about to hit a big downturn," I could support this in any number of ways that narrow what I really mean by the statement. Let's say I use a quotation to support my claim, and the expert says something like "There is a Venture Capital bubble that is about to pop – too many $1B companies at valuation have not played out that way in the stock market, and too many tech companies are built on false assumptions. It's widely regarded that there is a bubble in the tech industry just as bad as the .com bubble, and when it pops it's going to crush the tech space."

In this example, the real claim I'm supporting is "the tech small business space is about to hit a big downturn," not "the economy" is. But just because my support doesn't really match my claim doesn't mean I'm not on to something. What the audience heard was that the tech space is about to have a crisis, and I will need to do all the following: expose that the expert never referenced the economy in general, analyze whether the tech space is worth considering, and evaluate the support the expert provided as to why the bubble is about to pop (there were three warrants: stock market valuations, false assumptions, and wide regard that there's a bubble).

Wow! So how do you flow all that? Here's what my flow for this section would actually look like, for just this particular argument.

Their Speech	My Next Speech
Economy	A2 (answer to): Economy
> VC bubble	1. Not E – Tech Only
> $1B valuations	2. Fearmongering
> stock mkt	3. Rhetoric, not data
> wide regard	4. Many valuations <$1B

How does that turn into a presentation?

Now let's look at the exact words I'd say when presenting the "My Next Speech" points above. Here are the words that would come out of your mouth, based solely on the four responses on the right.

> "Next my opponent claimed the economy was heading towards a cliff. I have four responses.
>
> First: not the economy. The support provided only referenced the technology sector. What about transportation, finance, healthcare, education, logistics, and so on? Tech space is the wild west, not "the economy," and its volatility is to be expected.
>
> Second: Fearmongering. This sort of expert says words like 'crush' and references the .com boom, but other than the scary big words, what's really there?
>
> Third: rhetoric, not data. The expert here provided zero example companies, statistics, or even explanation as to why stock market

valuations matter – who cares if the stock market values a company less than its investors first did?

Fourth: Many valuations are sub-one-billion. Only some companies ever make it that high, but plenty of companies do well in mere hundreds of millions. It sounds like this expert made a couple bad investments is all.

So you can see, neither did my opponent prove the economy is in decline, nor did the quoted expert really even prove we should fear the tech space's bubble. Don't pass the plan because of the economy."

The words you say string together the outline you've built.

3rd – Key Appeals.

It's crucial to keep track of what has the most impact on your audience. Typically, this will be some sob story, an emotional hook, or some key statement at the beginning or end of a speech. One of my favorite tactics is to turn key appeals back against my opponent. Too many debaters just take these hits as granted, but usually they are weaker than they seem if you think for a sec "it's really, really important for me to re-wire the audience's thinking on that one." If you can deflate the items that had the highest impact, your audience will even do a little work for you on the less important things your opponent said.

I remember one round I debated where we failed to do this and it really hurt us. It was in college and my partner and I were debating an immigration resolution that year. Our opponents were two girls who apparently had been born in Asia. They ran a case to change the Constitution to allow foreign-born U.S. citizens to run for President. In the 1AR, the opening was about how the speaker and her partner had political aspirations but would never be able to run for President, even though they were U.S. Citizens born to U.S. Citizen parents. It was a gigantic sob story.

We didn't even respond to the story, because it wasn't "proving an argument" on the flow. (This was a year where I was too technical as a debater) Even though we demolished our opponents' overall proof for the case, had a huge disadvantage that was never even addressed, and were superior speakers and debaters in general, we lost this round because the judge couldn't bear to stop these girls from the chance of running for President.

If you can't address the heart of the matter, no matter how it was organized when presented, you will likely fail to grab the heart of your audience. And you, as we did then, will deserve to lose the debate.

Instead, we should have tackled this appeal head on and said what we were thinking.

4th – Drops and Explosions.

You're looking for what I'd call the "shape" of arguments. You can visually identify the shape of arguments just by looking at the ink on the page. I've even had some judges say "you didn't put enough ink on that" or "there was so much ink there, it was impossible to overcome."

If there is one point where your opponents have given seven responses, while there's another point where they haven't even acknowledged your argument, you shouldn't treat these arguments equally. Here are your strategic options:

- Argue that the dropped point was *the more important point* of the two, and simply jettison the other argument
- Put *equal weight* on the argument they treated heavily, and lightly use the dropped argument

The terrible option, but unfortunately the one that most linear debaters take, is this: continue to emphasize each argument equally. That makes no strategic sense. Can you see why? If you lose the one argument, you're going to need a pretty major comeback – so either win it or lose it and outweigh it. In either case, change your emphasis to whichever strategy you've chosen.

All the debaters I coach will tell you that my favorite moment is when an opponent fails to address a point (such as the weighing mechanism, or even one key example). That's because rather than complaining "they dropped my argument," I'll expose why that's bad. I'll say "here are three reasons it was the most important argument, and why you should cast your ballot and make your decision on the basis of this alone," if possible.

(If it's not possible, I shouldn't have been running the argument. One only should run "winning arguments," and visualizing yourself making just such a statement as above is a good way to tell if you're about to run a winning argument or not.)

So rather than complain about omission from our opponents, we exploit omission... unless, of course, they were right to ignore something irrelevant. We probably should do that as well, though it's best to mention why something is irrelevant.

So use your flow to identify priorities in the round, including omissions.

Flowing Advice to Ignore: Perfection

We cannot conclude our discussion of flowing without an inoculation against bad advice you will certainly receive. Assuming you learned the lesson from no-flow-boy, this advice is not an excuse for laziness, but a prescription for excellence: make your flow work for you, don't work for your flow.

Many coaches, and even several authors of debate books, have never debated competitively. And some who have do not keep it up (a sad omission, in my opinion, if debate is such a lifelong skill). As a result, their perspective of flowing is different than the practitioners. They are used to one role: listening. As a judge, general audience member, or coach, their use of the flow is from the seat not the lectern.

Of course their flows look better. Some of these coaches will tell you to perfect your flowing, with exacting rules and regulations of lines, colors, boxes, numbers, labels, and so on. This is garbage.

What your audience hears is what comes out of your mouth. They don't look at the organization of your personal notes. Too many debaters spend too much time making immaculate flows in the debate round, rather than using the flow as a tool to listen and prepare responses.

Here are some things that actually happen with great debaters:

- Stop flowing or even listening for a minute because a brilliant argument is in your mind and you just have to put words to it before it's gone. That's a huge risk, but if you've got a partner you'll warn them and steal their notes in a sec. Use this sparingly.
- Rip off a sheet and turn your flow sideways to plan a rebuttal. You're going to flow your opponent's most recent two speeches in the left side margin, because you're focusing on what your points and only listening for key round-swaying info now that it's rebuttals (I do this all the time, and am known for better rebuttals).
- Reorganize all the points, or scribble your real responses on a sticky note.
- Stop flowing on your own notepad for a second because you're going to write "AT: [next argument]" and write several responses for your partner, because your partner is digging through your printed materials.

I wrote this section of the book during a tournament weekend. I texted several national-class debaters, asking them to send a picture of their flowpads from their rounds. I've also included my own from two recent rounds. The point isn't the exact words on them, if you can even read them, but to see that the "perfect" system of flowing we're all taught isn't exactly how it plays out in-round. Accomplishing the objectives of flowing is more important than flowing.

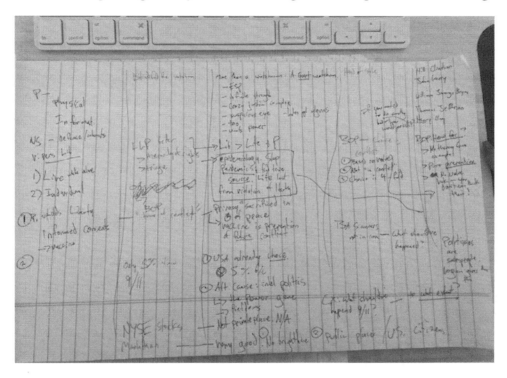

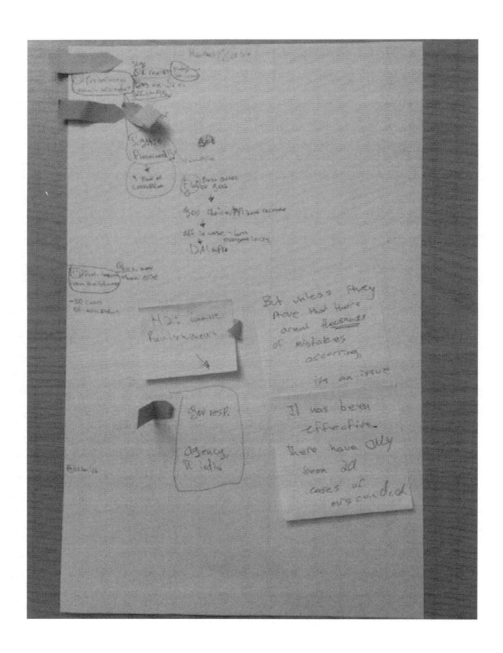

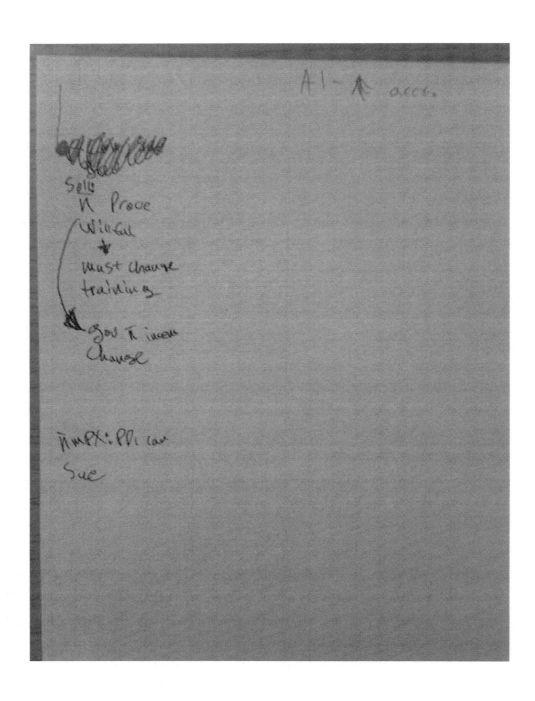

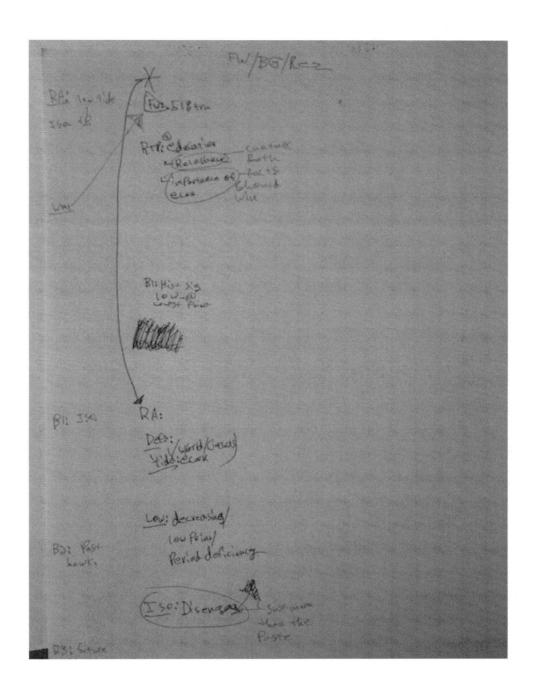

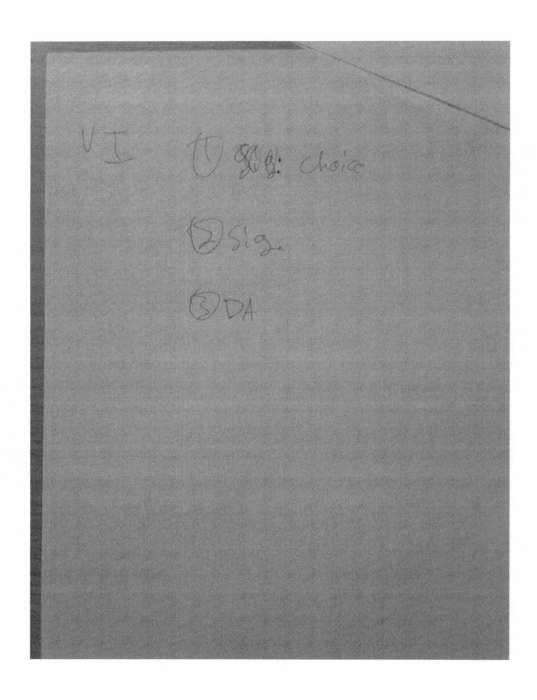

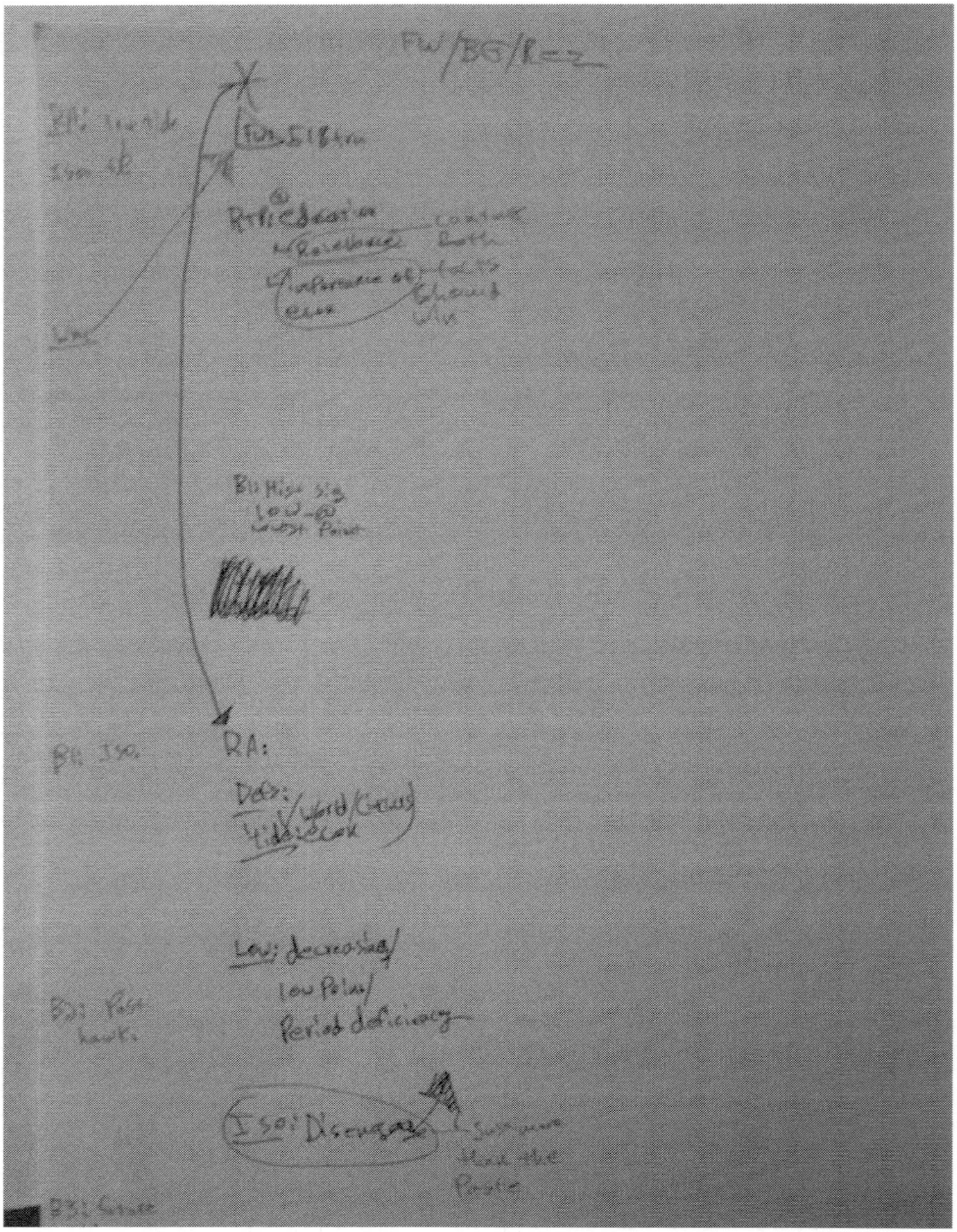
RA:
Low: decreasing/

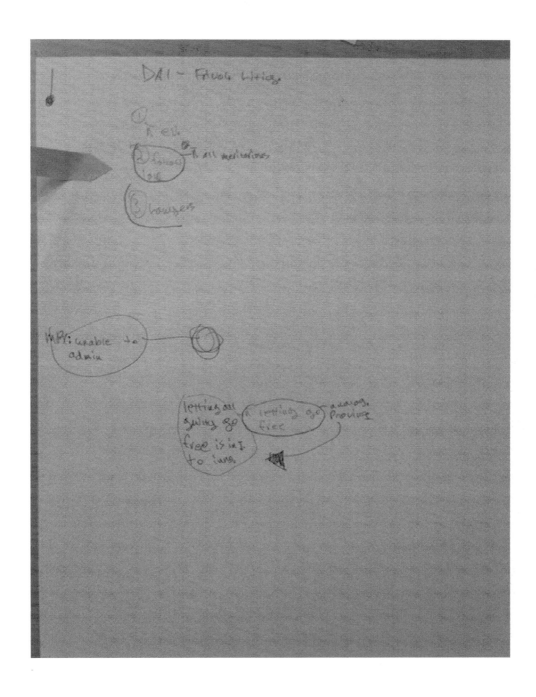

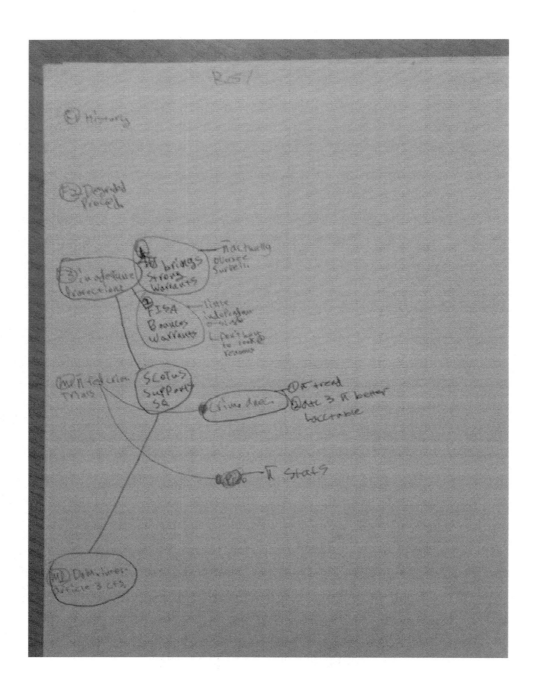

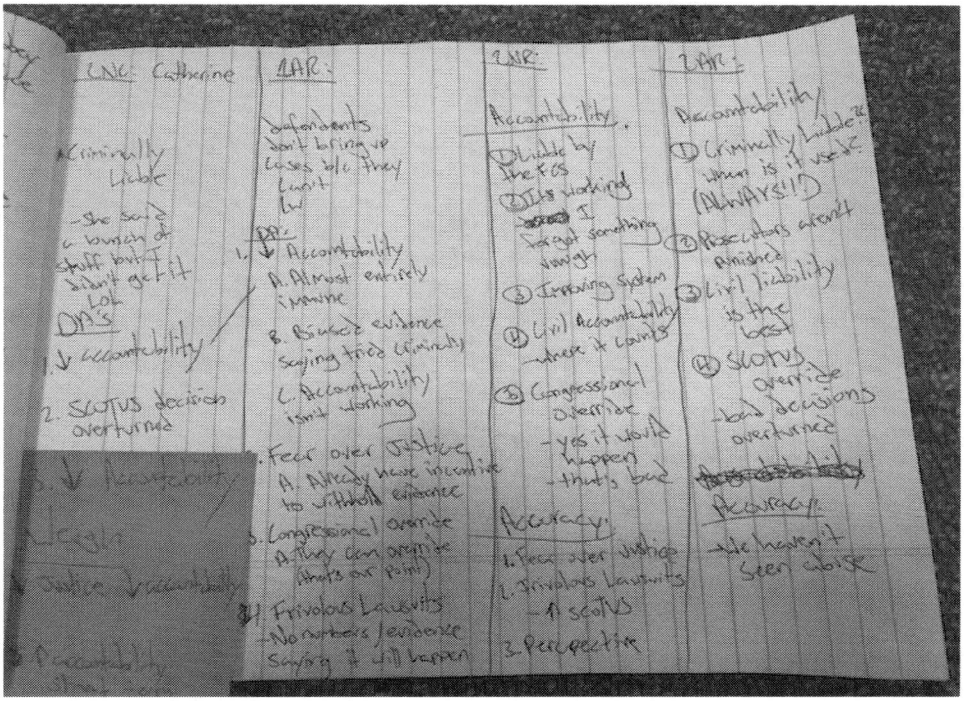
1NC: Catherine
1AR:
2NR:
2AR:
Criminally Liable
DA's
1. ↓ Accountability
2. SCOTUS decision overturned
Defendants don't bring up cases b/c they can't
1. ↓ Accountability
A. Almost entirely immune
C. Accountability isn't working
Fear over Justice
A. Already have incentive to withhold evidence
Congressional override
Frivolous Lawsuits
- No numbers / evidence saying it will happen
Accountability
Improving System
Civil Accountability
Congressional override
- yes it would happen
- that's bad
Accuracy
1. Fear over Justice
2. Frivolous Lawsuits
3. Perspective
Accountability
Criminally Liable?
(ALWAYS!!)
Prosecutors aren't punished
Civil liability is the best
SCOTUS override
- bad decisions overturned
Accuracy
- We haven't seen abuse

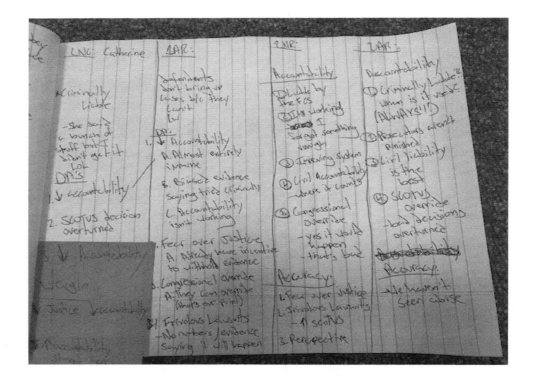

And now let's bring it all together into real life. The following five images are my actual flow from an extremely intense conflict-resolution business meeting that I recently had. Nothing to do with debate competitions, except every skill from debate being used in the real world. The conversation went so well and ended healthy because of this method, and I was able to stay organized and collected.

Jared — Challenging vs. Being Heard

> Same page

"Never ack again" — good to ask

— Ask as a learner
— Not as a challenger

> Not "why are we doing it this way?"

Reagan:

> Be direct:

> Not assumptive; have we got

> learn.

$ 2 mos: tone Δed from curious to challenge

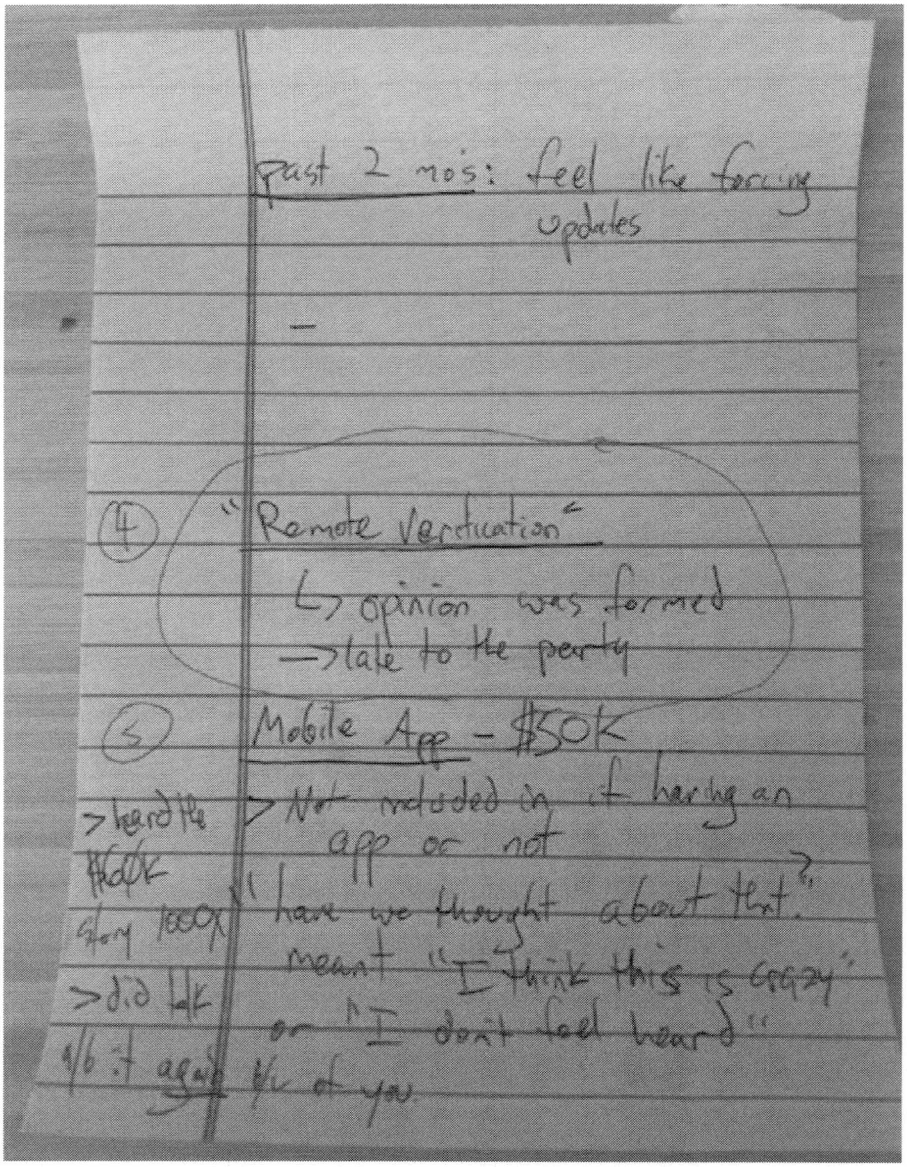
past 2 mo's: feel like forcing updates

—

④ "Remote Verification"

↳ opinion was formed

→ late to the party

⑤ Mobile App – $50K

> Not included in if having an app or not

"have we thought about that?"

meant "I think this is crazy" or "I don't feel heard" b/c of you.

> heard the [?]60K story 1000x

> did 60K

9/6 it again

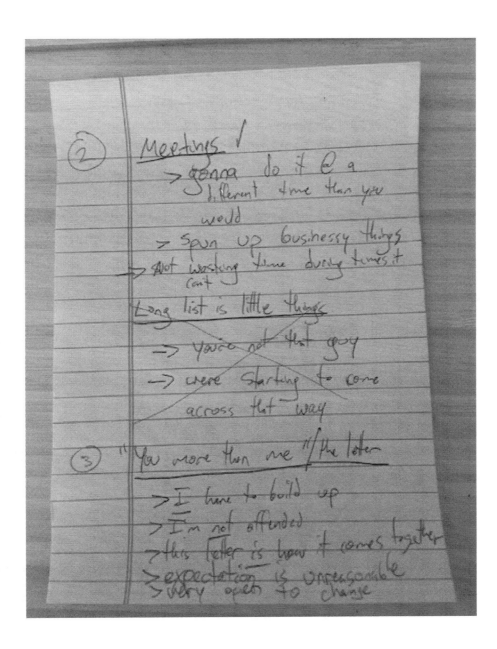

1. "Ask for feedback" on the product

   "Let me in"

   ↳ Perception that you're not being let in

   → ask how, rather than debate

2. @ Convention: would've liked a heads up. Caught me off guard

   → I'm not doing my own thing

   → KR ← I told you so x

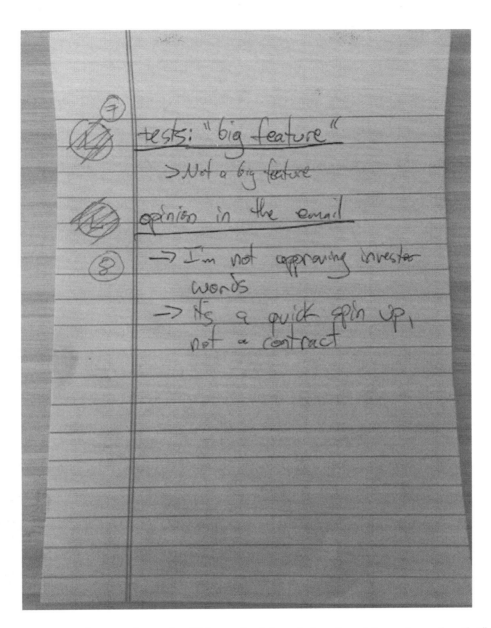

Don't learn flowing from the "I haven't debated, but I watch and coach a lot" perspective; learn it from the debater's side of the lectern: it's messier than your audience will ever know. You need to pursue the principles and deliver a great speech, not turn in your flowsheet to win a flowing competition.

How to Practice Flowing

Real simple: do it. Here are things you can flow:

- Preparing the outline of ideas you've got for a writing project, or any project really.
- Listen to a lecture, TED talk, sermon, or great speech, and flow what was said. If you want to take this to the next level, write your "responses" to the right.
- Take a blog, speech, or video from some idea you oppose, and prepare your own outline to respond.
- Grab a debate on YouTube and decide you're one of the middle speakers (you're going to partner with someone on the ol' tube). Flow your opponents and partner, and prepare your own speech. Then see what the "real" partner did.

Conclusion

The flow is the crucial listening tool for not only debaters, but people who have conversations with other people and wish to respond. I've even had a week-long conversation/debate with someone at work in a google spreadsheet where we wrote every idea and then responded out to the right for column after column until resolving each issue. Flowing works, but your style of flowing needs to be adaptive rather than static.

Learn some modes that work for you, then focus on achieving the outcome: listening and being persuasive.

Chapter 8. How to Be Persuasive (Theory)

Do you hope to be persuasive? Or, do you hope to get people to do what you want?

These two goals are related, yet not the same.

Persuasion opens the audience's minds to rational thoughts, leading them to choose what is best. Manipulation, on the other hand, aims to close the audience's minds towards all except a single choice, where the audience gives in to what the speaker wants.

Manipulation succeeds for a variety of reasons: urgency, fear, lack of knowledge, clouded judgment, "us-versus-them" rhetoric that paints "them" as heretical, greed, and the relative power of the speaker over the audience.

This chapter will teach you how to persuade, not how to manipulate. Because our culture struggles with identifying the difference between the two, we will start with several general concepts from classical rhetoric, before diving into the mechanics of persuasion. The final portion will teach you how to "make a case" for any idea, which is the beginning point of persuasion.

Once you learn this, you'll be ready to start debating!

How Persuasion Values People: Removal of Self

Modern rhetoric expert Jay Heinrichs wrote an amazing book called, *Thank You for Arguing: What Aristotle, Lincoln, and Homer Simpson Can Teach Us About The Art of Persuasion.* I recommend reading this after you've spent six months on your first job. Jay describes how there are few rhetorical no-nos, but the ones that do exist serve as "pitfalls and nastiness that can bollix an argument." Chief among them? Turning an argument into a fight.

Types of Discussions

- **Arguing** is how humans reason to conclusions.
- **Fighting** is how humans interact with pre-determined conclusions and no openness to the concept that there may be another conclusion.
- **Persuasion** is how someone guides a mind from point A to point B (the conclusion).
- **Lecturing** is how someone guides a mind to predetermined conclusions on the assumption that the listener has already assented to learning. When no questions are allowed, to boot, we can call that "Preaching."
- **Teaching** is how someone guides a mind to conclusions, using persuasion.
- **Coaching** is how someone unlocks the inner potential of a person to become the best version of themselves.
- **Conversation** is a two-way discussion where "the point" is the people in the conversation, and no particular person has the floor. Any conversation can turn into an argument, lecture, or fight, at any time.

If you are a news host, it seems your job is to ensure a conversation becomes a fight.

A conversational presentation style is preferable because it requires the attitude, language, and tone of someone as willing to be persuaded as they are persuasive. If you've obviously already made up your mind but think the audience should change theirs, then you're not treating others as you want to be treated. You're lecturing now, and in danger of preaching (talking "at" people). Assuming this role, which places two equal human beings in a position where one is "greater" and the other is "lesser," is what leads to fighting.

The lecturer may never know his audience's thoughts because there's no platform to share them, but in conversation you each have equal footing, whereas lecturing or preaching often goes straight to fighting.

Why? Because fighting is about a person's assertion, not the substance of the idea. That's why I often teach professional businesspeople that "successful speakers must be self-sacrificial," and why I admonish politicians to "love your audience." Anything less may leave you feeling like you said words that were good, but typically you've done no real persuasion, unless you count the people who already agreed with you in the first place.

So in order to be persuasive, you have to drop the defense. You're dropping the same defense that you want your audience to drop and replace it with a willingness to listen and consider arguments that may even lead you to a different conclusion than one with which you began.

That's why the best debaters are peacemakers. They realize that peace is required to even open a forum for persuasion. Most debaters never learn this, and are merely argumentative (a word that means "cause fights").

So the **first key to being truly persuasive to people who don't already agree with you is to drop the armor.** You have to be willing to hear the other side and go that way if it is sensible. (Just wait until you watch an obstinate cross-examinee refuse to assent to what's reasonable, and you'll see what I mean.) Enhance your credibility with a disposition of persuadability.

The **second key is that you need to listen well.** How many times have you felt someone's argument against you misrepresented what you said? Misrepresentation or uncharitable interpretation of what others say ignites a fight from a discussion. The first person to speak feels offended that her words weren't heard correctly, and then assumes her opponent is twisting her words deliberately. A fight is now on the way.

In everyday conversation and meetings as well as in cross-examination in a competitive debate round, the same advice holds true: listen with empathy.

Stephen R. Covey captures it well in his book *7 Habits of Highly Successful People:* "Most people do not listen with the intent to understand; they listen with the intent to reply."

Listening only to reply shreds the deliberative aspect of argument. It's a good way to lose your own credibility, guarantee non-creativity in a business meeting, and ruin a friendship or marriage. Not to mention failing to genuinely help an audience wrestling with a topic. Listening to reply is about you, not the idea.

So before we talk about being persuasive, we must work on daily habits to help us become good listeners, and as a result, good persuaders.

Three Life Habits of the Truly Persuasive

- Always work towards a conversational disposition, where it is clear that you are someone who may be persuaded
- Always demonstrate active listening, that you understand more than what was said but also what was meant, and treat it respectfully enough to have considered it well before opening your mouth to respond

- And most of all, always avoid personalization of the debate so that it is about you vs. the other person

Here's a negative example. I just went to a random online forum to find a long argumentative thread, and found my way into a passionate discussion about something related to Universities and policy. I found this at the top of one of the replies:

> Professor Palczewski,
>
> I'm pleased that you find my comments "amusing" but I thought I was expressing a "serious concern". The present wording creates serious problems because it is difficult to comply with without the person in charge deciding that the Feb 8th date in the rule as currently written is meaningful but that the Feb 1st date is an arbitrary guideline.

It goes on. (At length.) But I draw your attention to this: when one side calls the other side's points "amusing," just like when Fox News commentators say they're "outraged" that someone can even think something else, at that moment, suddenly it's no longer about the substance, but about the person. **To de-escalate personalized discussions, we have to completely avoid judging/demeaning the position and simply respond to the position.** It's obvious that someone DOES think that thing, so acting like it's outrageous for them to do so only creates a mile-high wall of separation that guarantees zero persuasion will occur.

Tactic: Build Up the "Other"

An Isaiah story...

> When I was an advanced debater in high school I actually lost several rounds to novice teams. We're talking about a junior in high school debating some

13-year-olds who don't use 50% of their speech time, don't make eye contact, and whose arguments are... poor.

Judges would say things like "too confident," or "you went for the jugular vein," and I would consistently get low speaker points in these novice opponent rounds, despite usually receiving tournament speaker awards when debating difficult opponents.

I spent time overcoming this challenge. By learning to debate novices, I learned essential skills for making peace. It has helped me in relationships, business, and leadership.

I've committed to a life habit called "Build UP the Other." Instead of calling silly arguments "silly," or blowing up their one weak point with seven responses, I learned a different approach to overcoming arguments that seem weak to me.

How to Refute Weak Arguments

1. **Build Up.** Before you tear down your opponent's idea, invest time building up his argument to something even better than it was, fully capturing all that was intended, even if imperfectly communicated. One of the trickiest parts of this is running a cross-examination where you build up your opponent's argument and say "so it seems like you're saying this, and that's because of that... which would mean this really bad thing for our case, right?" And then you don't refute it right there or cause them to admit something else – you don't make them mouth the words of their own defeat.

2. **Empathize.** Admit that parts of this argument are challenging/good and bring attention to the most important parts.

3. **Walk the Journey to Your Side.** Only now defeat the argument, with a tone of "having considered their side well and initially finding it

persuasive, I actually ended up eventually concluding something different."

Remember how non-persuasive communication pits person versus person, instead of idea versus idea? Building up a weak opponent's argument improves the relative stature of the opponent, so that the following exchange of ideas does not appear as bullying, oppressive, or somehow using personal position or authority as the basis of persuasion.

What You Accomplish by Building UP the Other

1. **Honor your opponent.** Your opponent doesn't feel demeaned or personally weakened because of your response. Instead of putting them down, you put them up above you for being reasonable and thoughtful.

2. **Gain credibility.** Your audience sees you spending the time to truly consider, so it doesn't seem like you've just been itching to "reply." Instead, you're quite reasonable.

3. **Consider alternatives.** By forcing yourself to see the best part of your opponent's position, you actually become a more in-depth thinker. You'll soon despise others less as you start to see that they really DO have some little nuggets of wisdom in their poorly expressed argument.

Let's take a quick look at how this might help your relationships, business skills, and leadership.

Relationships

Drs. John and Julie Gottman are internationally famous for their research into relational communications. One of their most crucial tips for dealing with conflict is this: when someone expresses how they feel offended, you cannot argue with them; instead, you need to express back to them how they feel, demonstrating you understand it.

Remember types of resolutions? "I feel" is subjective and non-debatable. Only when someone agrees that you understand and empathize with their viewpoint will they feel your next response is not putting them lower than you. So don't argue with people's perceptions; build them up before changing them. When you do, sometimes you will notice how it is you that was changed.

Business

There is a centuries-old cycle of innovation: large business is arrogant about its own position, doesn't take a competitor seriously, then loses later on when small innovative team improves on the behemoth's idea. The first product that an innovative challenger puts out there won't be the best and final product they're going to out-compete with – so trashing it in your own minds and saying how it can never catch up, and mocking the competition is a pretty surefire way to get beaten in the long run.

Instead, see the strengths of competitors and even make them stronger in your own mind, because surely there is more to them that you don't know about. Only after you have done this should you consider responding with charity and seriousness.

Leadership

In Boy Scouts Leadership Training (circa 2002, anyways) they teach the number 1 rule of leadership is "empathy." I agree. Poor leaders tell people what to do, listen to reply (don't listen), and without knowing it constrict the great potential inside their teams until it is limited to only the ideas that flow out of their own brain.

Great companies, like Pixar, ensure that titles mean nothing in the ideas room.

Seeing through the perspective of each employee is the only way to create a safe harbor for the best ideas that will together collide and lead towards success.

Any great leader recognizes that innovation occurs after dozens of failures, and so always looks through the eyes of the team and builds up ideas to something better than the way those ideas were expressed.

Three Essential Classical Rhetoric Concepts

You need to know a couple of concepts from the ancient tradition of rhetoric to complete your mindset towards persuasion as something other than fighting.

Rhetoric Concept 1: "Identification"

"But here's the thing," says rhetoric expert Jay Heinrichs, "persuasion isn't about me. It's about the beliefs and expectations of my audience...Get the group to identify with you and you have won half the persuasive battle."

The audience needs to be able to find a tiny bit of themselves inside of you. The audience will only really listen once they can identify with you about something.

You've probably even seen this in action as a frustrating fallacy! I bet you have a relative who trusts a political candidate because of **one thing** that person did or said. After that point of identification, which other candidates have failed to create with this relative, your family member seems willing to ignore all the downsides of the candidate.

But should we expect anything different? It's impossible to be persuaded by someone when you don't see anything the same way. Thus, the great rhetors—whether they know they're doing it or not—implement tactics of identification.

Here are a few ways to identify with your audience.

- **Identify Top Risks.** Imagine you are your audience. Think of what you're trying to communicate as they might see it. Now identify your top two riskiest points, in the sense that these arguments may be less persuasive than other ones. Now tell yourself: these are actual risks, not "unreasonable doubts" from my audience and address them accordingly.

- **Ask About Your Audience.** Whenever I'm invited to speak or have to build a marketing deck or a web page, I always ask: "who is the audience?" Just imagine how differently you would give a presentation if the audience were 55-year-old executives from the automotive industry versus 19-year-old college students studying history. When your audience is super mixed, who they are isn't the right question. Instead ask: "why are they here?"

- **Demonstrate Commonality.** Without being cheesy ("Here are three ways that I am like you..."), help your audience see themselves in you. For example, say things like "you're probably thinking..." and "you may be wondering..." because these phrases will force you to say something that should be matching their perspective, not yours.

An audience identifies with you when they feel what it's like to see life through your eyes. They'll only do that if you work to see life through theirs.

Rhetoric Concept 2: "Movement"

Imagine you're speaking right now in a conversation. Think about the listeners. What are they doing? Nothing?

No, it's something. But what?

Being changed. (Well... assuming they're actually listening, and not "listening to reply." But then it's not really a conversation, is it?)

In physics, any change can be thought of as some sort of spent energy. When no change is happening, inertia. When change is happening, energy. (Work with me here, math/science people.) Energy is movement. Something went from one place to somewhere else. If it went back to where it started, it still went somewhere along the way.

Persuasion is just like this. Assuming your audience is listening, you're always causing them to move.

- Perhaps the move is temporary, and you bring them on a journey from what they previously thought right back to thinking that even more staunchly.
- Perhaps the move is unrelated to your message. For example, a boring talk can cause nodding heads while minds retreated off to some beach paradise or cynical list of one-liner Tweets about how silly this is.
- Perhaps the move is real, and you've put your audience in a new intellectual home. Google "Persuasive Inoculation Theory" to learn more about ensuring they stay there once you're gone.

In sum, a key part of persuading is adopting the mindset of a "mover." The true rhetor makes a lifelong commitment to only move other humans towards the good.

As a consequence of thinking of persuasion as "movement," you are more likely to adopt some of the following mindsets towards communication:

1. **Audience Focus** – the purpose of your communication isn't to unload the words in your brain, but to move an audience. That you have a mass of things to say may not be relevant, and may hurt your

own goal. We all recognize when someone enjoys hearing themselves talk more than moving an audience.

2. **There's a Starting Point** – if you're moving an audience, it's crucial to figure out where that audience is right now. Are you moving from point A to point Z or from point D to point Z? Depending on where your audience starts, their pathway to Z may be different. Poor speakers just provide their own path from A to Z without considering that others have different starting points. Asking questions before speaking, and analyzing listener cues, are the two best methods for discovering starting points.

3. **There's a Path** – the key to persuasion isn't having a compelling conclusion that you strongly believe. The key is to figure out EXACTLY what led to that conclusion: a series of assumptions, principles, experiences, reasons, and priorities. Each person has all that stuff. What we must learn is how to reveal that path to our audience, and the right sequence and words to help us do it. That's why deep thought precedes effective speech.

Now let's exemplify these mindsets at work in some examples from "real life" and debate.

- **Job Interview:** Instead of merely answering questions asked about your skills and fit for the position, you begin the interview by asking "what internal challenges or pains led to the creation of this job role in the first place?" The answer will give you a much deeper finishing point, originating in your audience's mind, and you can work your audience down that path.
- **Product Design:** Many people think that product design is about creating what you believe is a great idea, and then hoping other people

like it and you can sell it. There is a method called Lean Startup, which takes an audience-focused approach to find a starting point and unveil a path. The key is to make a minimum viable product – the smallest possible feature set required to gain a buck – and then go learn why people do or don't buy it, and then light up the path to continued development of this product into the full-blossomed idea you had in mind, but usually on a somewhat different path and described in the same words your audience finds powerful. Tools used here include before/during/after customer journey maps, customer interviews, and other audience-focused activities.

- **Debate Round:** At nationals 2003, my debate partner and I ran the 23rd version of our case for the year. The entire year we argued for free trade with sub-Saharan African nations, but the final version was radically different than the original version. We learned the most common objections to free trade (jobs lost, wage impact, competition with U.S. businesses), and learned to overcome them. Other debaters often dropped a case because there were strong arguments against it, but we dug in to understand the root assumptions that audiences hold that made free trade unpersuasive. In our final version, we framed the free trade debate as a conflict between protectionist thinking and free market economics. We chose free market economics as the "starting point" for our audiences, and walked them down a path to free trade. There's one last point that must be made when discussing movement: **you don't own the path, you're just on the path.** Persuasive people recognize that they traveled a journey to some conclusion, and the journey and its map may be clearer to them, but is still something they traveled, not something they invented. When you create a case for an idea, the idea exists without you. And you being

"defeated" in some argument doesn't defeat the idea for all time...
perhaps another can help folks walk the path.When you think well of
"movement" in rhetoric, you will begin to recognize that the speaker
merely connects an audience with an idea. Both audience and speaker
observe that idea together, as third parties.If the audience is required
to assent to you, your ownership of the idea, their "wrongness" or
your "rightness," then you now stand as a barrier to the destination at
the end of the path. And that's selfish communicating. And that's what
most people do. And that's what the master overcomes, by removing
self as a barrier on the persuasive path of motion.

Rhetoric Concept 3: "Stasis"

Stasis identifies the issues that must be resolved to complete an argument.

When two parties disagree, there is no rule that they must disagree on
everything. In fact, it is guaranteed that they do agree on something: the issue is
worth discussing, both parties have a right to speak, facts and reasoning should
govern the discussion, and so on.

You can rapidly spot an unreasonable party to a disagreement as the one who
is unwilling to agree to anything the other party says, even when patently true
or obvious. As an audience, we think of that person as having some personal
motive of gain influencing their decision to put reason aside, or as being driven
by emotions rather than thoughts.

More common than unreasonableness, however, is disjointed disagreement.
That's when both parties disagree on a conclusion, but their reasons for
disagreeing don't actually clash. Here's a simplistic illustration:

> You: I can't stand country.
> Her: I love country music. Why can't you stand it?

You: The celebrities all lead such fake, plastic lives.

Her: Well what's a specific song you dislike? I think so many songs have deep meaning, and sound good.

You: Taylor Swift and Carrie Underwood sold out – they're terrible role models.

What's going on here? Why does it seem like you are talking past each other? Because there is no stasis – no central agreement, even about what the disagreement is.

- You are talking about country as an industry
- She is talking about country as purely the music

So how could you take a step back and get on the same page? Arguably, it's definitional: what is "country" – the music, or the industry? She may actually completely agree that the industry is awful, and you may actually agree that the songs are good.

Try this: "Wait a sec... I think country should be judged by the entirety of the industry, not just the sound of the music it produces." Now you've identified where you think the original point of disagreement flows from, and stand a chance of bringing the conversation on track. You can both discuss the current crux, and then move on or not, or agree to disagree. All three scenarios avoid the conversation you were having:

- Neither of you can agree with how to judge "country," so you then carry on a conversation about its parts: the people and the music.
- You both agree that country is the industry: now you weigh the potential pros and cons of music and people in it, and perhaps both of you agree about ALL the facts there.
- You both agree that country music as music can be one discussion, and you'll talk about the industry later (or just forget about it because

obviously any industry that sings about its own name so much is going to be self-absorbed).

Whew. You've solved the primary reason that many conversations are so terrible by identifying that the core of your disagreement wasn't actually what either of you were discussing. Cultivating the eyes to see this is more than critical thinking, it's a habit of wisdom that can lead to conflict reduction and refocus argumentative conversations towards more productive turf.

Stasis is the classical rhetor's method of finding the crux of any disagreement. Sometimes the argument must become as core as discussing whether "this topic is important," or "should we use reasoning and words to decide what to do," or even "are we making a decision, or simply toying with ideas?" These are three assumptions – the topic is important, reasoning is how we'll proceed, and our discussion leads to a decision – that actually underpin most discussions anyway, but may need to be named in order to proceed. Here are some things that happen when these are not shared:

- **This topic is important.** While you are attempting earnestly to discuss the issue, your fellow conversant is simply attempting to exit the conversation or is belittling the points you make.
- **We should use reasoning.** For example, if someone is holding to the conclusion because they believe themselves superior in experience and status, someone attempting to dissuade them through use of reason does not have a common ground yet and will need to back up a little to find some.
- **We're making a decision.** If one person is "playing devil's advocate" and the other person believes the discussion will lead to a real decision at the end of it, you may see escalation in emotion simply because the stasis was actually around the nature of the conversation, less than its substance.

In a debate or conversation, I typically use stasis with phrases like these:

- The crux of the issue is really whether or not [we believe Justice demands a restorative component, in addition to punitive].
- The debate isn't [over the importance of presenting a simple brand], it's [whether or not my approach is actually simple].
- Our disagreement doesn't center on [what we should do], but on [why we should do it].
- The root cause of our disagreement is actually definitional: we don't mean the same thing by [comprehensive] – let's hash that out and then see if we still disagree.

Thus, cultivating the ability to identify stasis is all about seeing the multiple areas of potential conflict in a discussion, noticing exactly which ones are actual areas of conflict and the order in which they should be addressed.

Classical Rhetoric provides us the following broad categories for stasis:

- Definition/Description – what is the nature of the issue and its meaning?
- Conjecture – what are the facts? Not the opinion or judgment of those facts, but the pure facts.
- Quality – the judgment of the issue (what we typically expect is the heart of a debate, but often is not).
- Solution – the merits of a plan to address an issue.

De-tangling a discussion that feels like a disagreement is often as simple as creating a sort of checklist of these items. For example, if you find yourself in a heated disagreement about a solution to a problem, perhaps back up and see if you share agreement on the nature of the problem.Sometimes even the basic definition of what is being discussed is at issue. For example, in business, to some "marketing" means arts and crafts and to others it is the department that knows the customers best and guides the entire business strategy. When discussing what "marketing" should do, it's essential to first determine which activities of marketing are under discussion.So use stasis to identify the real points of conflict, and then focus on those, not on the broad and general nature of being in a state of disagreement.Try identifying the stasis in the following examples, and you'll learn how to be a problem solver!

Example 1: Business Decision at Corporate Gifting Inc.

Customer Support Rep: "Our coffee product is just getting us such terrible reviews, and I'm tired of being yelled at."

CEO: "Well tell the product team what they need to do to fix it!"

Customer Support Rep: "I don't know how to fix it, I just know that it's broken. We're much better at all of our non-consumable products, like keychains, mugs, and hacky sacks."

CEO: "I know what we're good at! I need what we're bad at to get better."

Product Manager: "I'm not going to just sit here and let customer support attack me! Maybe they need to get behind the product and learn how to actually support it."

Customer Support Rep: "I'm not trying to make you look bad! It's just that this product makes US look bad!"

Stasis: The wise CEO would at this point "go back" to some deeper issues, and not let the conversation escalate. It's covering too many issues at a time. What should the CEO identify as the crux?

CEO: "Hey, we all want our company to succeed, to please our customers, and to have a good team. No one disagrees on these points and we're all friends here. It looks like the root cause of disagreement may actually begin with whether we should offer this product in the first place. Let's start there – why is it essential for us to provide this product?"

Now the CEO can help guide the discussion to its next step, which is for or against a specific question. If the decision is to keep the product line, then the next question is to identify whether improvement will come from product changes, how it is marketed, and/or how it is supported. If the decision is to abandon the product line, then the next question is how to shut it down with the least cost to the company.

Notice how non-conflict-oriented this sort of discussion could be. That's because it's depersonalized when both sides can agree on exactly what the disagreement point is, and are willing to discuss it. Usually stasis is exactly that.

Example 2: Political Candidates

When we started writing this book, Barack Obama was in his first term. Now Donald Trump has just won primaries in major states in the 2016 election cycle. Who knows when you're reading this (post-neo-Trumptik Ameriland or same ol' USA as before, who knows?), so please kindly play along and just learn the lesson.

> Friend1: "After much research, I've decided that I plan to vote for Donald Trump."
> Friend2: "How could you support a fascist who has run multiple businesses into the ground and used bankruptcy to protect businesses? I'm offended."

This interaction is doomed from the start. While we could notice that Friend2 does not start with listening and understanding, doesn't start by learning or establishing shared assumptions, doesn't allow the discussion to be about ideas by stating offense to make it personal, and provides a series of impossibly loaded questions... what we shall choose to notice regarding stasis is that Friend2 simply assumed the following:

- a. Friend1 agrees that Trump's statements make him a fascist
- b. Friend1 agrees that Trump's running multiple businesses into the ground makes him a poor leader, given obvious successes as well
- c. Friend1 agrees that using legal methods of business protection make one bad, rather than good
- d. Friend1 believes that these qualities represent poor President skills, given unmentioned positives and the other candidates that may become President instead

If we can assume that Friend1 legitimately has done some research, we could, in fact, conclude that Friend2 is the one doing the offending, for treating Friend1 as an irrational imbecile and engaging in a conversation without listening or respecting. And this is probably what will happen, as both parties huff and puff and stay offended and plug their ears singing lalalala as they wait for a spare moment to reply. (Ever been in a conversation like this?)

Good thing you're there to make peace. That's what real debaters can do, because they can rapidly identify points of stasis and therefore de-escalate the conflict.

You: "We all share the premise that doing something good for our country, and not tanking it, is valuable. Nobody is trying to offend anyone if they've simply decided that certain facts seem to indicate one candidate is best for our common goal. We share that goal, right? (heads nod) If we're really interested in having a discussion, it looks like the core issue is to start with what makes a good President at this time. Then we can talk through each of Trump's qualities. But I have to say, the first question I'd really like us to answer is this: are we really interested in having an open discussion about who to vote for?

Because that means listening to both sides and actually being willing to consider what someone else is saying... do you all want to do that?"

You have properly identified not only the content of stasis (qualities that make a good President at this time), but the moment of stasis – perhaps neither side is actually interested in genuinely discussing (arguing, debating, conversing, whatever you want to call it) the issue. If, instead, each side simply wants to state what they like about their side and then revile the other side, you don't have a discussion or debate on your hands and it's not even worth proceeding, since both sides already share this assumption: we won't change our own minds.

As you can see, successful debaters will identify the most recent point of agreement (shared assumption) and the next point of disagreement (stasis), which is usually a yes/no sort of question that leads towards a path of other yes/no questions, one at a time.

Learning to observe in the storm of a conversation the linear path of assumptions and ideas that lead to a conclusion is perhaps THE most essential critical thinking habit you can pick up from debate. It will make you a great leader and peacemaker, and transfers to every area of life.

Now with the concepts of Identification, Movement, and Stasis in place, let us get down to the mechanics of persuasion proper.

Chapter 9. How to Be Persuasive (Mechanics)

Then how to we guide people to change their minds? More precisely, how do we guide people to realize that they actually think something different?

Work from Shared Assumptions

As you probably have guessed from our discussion of Stasis, true persuasion begins with shared assumptions and works towards conclusions. I think of it as a linear workflow, like this:

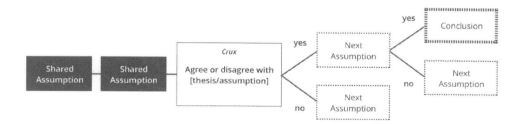

On the far right is the ultimate conclusion for which you're aiming. On the left is some point of common ground that provides a starting point. Your goal is to establish the logical links from the starting point of shared assumption, towards the conclusion. Each step towards the conclusion creates a new shared assumption.

Here's an example with content.

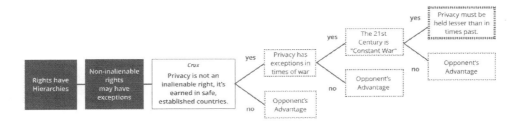

The "Opponent's Advantage" boxes mean that events took your argument off track from its intended destination. That doesn't mean the discussion is over! First of all, consider going down your opponent's track for awhile. But creatively think how to get back on track with your argument – the opponent's advantage may simply be a short detour. Be open to the idea that your conclusion is no longer available, however, or you will instantly become non-persuasive.

In debate you might hear this concept spoken of in terms of claims and warrants. A claim is a conclusion; warrants are reasons the claim is true. Warrants are the assumptions and ideas that lead to the conclusion. It is manipulative rather than persuasive to try to get someone to agree with your claims, without getting agreement to the warrants that support your claim.

Now here's a fun point: sometimes people can arrive at the same conclusion for entirely different reasons. If you cannot get to a conclusion via one pathway, sometimes it's worth trying another! A different shared assumption may lead to the same result.

Just remember this: the points should progress one discrete step at a time... you want to avoid dumping "everything" all at once. A progression of thought gets your audience beginning to process in advance, doing work for you, and ultimately arriving at the conclusion before you put words to the thought.

In any case, here are the key observations for arguing from shared assumptions:

1. Start from a Common Source.

Imagine an argument laid out in a flowchart like the one above. If you were to argue two steps in, but do not share assumptions to the left, you will only talk past your audience. Many presenters fail for not working from a point of common ground, even as simple as a shared goal or agreement that the issue is worth a conversation.

2. Focus on the crux.

Think stasis, from the previous chapter. The point of current disagreement is the most important point at the moment. You don't have to gain commitment to points further down the chain, yet, and don't even have to mention them. Sometimes these further points — the conclusions your audience will ultimately find inescapable – can distract your opponents and build false resistance.

If you walked into a business and said, "I am going to argue for your abolition," you will get much less traction than if you start with "I am going to argue that customers in your industry deserve the best solution available, because it's often a matter of life or death." Assuming all agree, the next question will be whether this company provides the best solution available. If it does not, the audience will be forced into contradiction if they do not either conclude to improve their solution (an "opponent's advantage" alternate conclusion) or abolish themselves (your conclusion). Identify the crux, and maximize your resources there.

3. You may be surprised.

Sometimes you will think that it's a four-link argument, but to your audience it's more like seven. As you discuss the points of stasis, you will begin to reveal why your opponents disagree, and realize that there may be sub-assumptions you didn't know before. How will you learn this? Because in this approach to persuasion, you have to listen and understand in order to progress.

Thus, a true listener will ultimately be more persuasive than someone who fails to listen and only argues for the conclusion. These people find themselves persuasive, but are not persuasive to others, because there are deeper assumptions. And that is the secret to persuasiveness: finding your audience's concerns and working with them, not simply unloading what was persuasive to you.

4. You can de-escalate conflict.

When you start with a shared assumption, it's like you and your audience or opponent already agree on something. How nice! Then that you diverge in some respect (the NEXT assumption, not the final conclusion) is a matter of interest – how is it that you go one way and me another? – not a matter of conflict.

The ultimate goal here is to get out of the way of the argument, and ultimately lead the audience to find that the end conclusion was what they thought all along, they just didn't know it yet. Now your opponent doesn't have to "admit defeat;" you simply were a teacher, not a conqueror. Arguing from shared assumptions ditches the "you're wrong, I'm right" mindset, replacing it with "you may lack info that I happen to have, and perhaps the opposite is true, let's see...".

So, what if you're always right about everything?

How do you persuade people when you're already always right?

Live in a cave and never talk to another human again.

Persuasion starts with this core shared assumption that makes someone reasonable: if there are strong enough arguments to the contrary, I will change my position. Not "you," but "I". If the person who aims to persuade is unwilling to listen, think, and consider, then on a stage this person should never be heard. This person is an information dictator (and possibly a real one!): do what I say because I said it, not because it's most reasonable. For if I were persuading you on the basis of reasonability, I would be open to doubting my position. On the contrary, if you expect your audience to have an open mind, you should lead by example.

Then why do unreasonable people often have followers? Unreasonable people have followers because the followers hope to gain something by it, the followers lack critical thinking skills (they aren't the kind of followers that YOU want), or the followers were already going wherever this person managed to get out in front. It's as easy to tell yourself you are persuasive when you've merely put words to what people already think as it is for a rich person to tell himself that he has true friends. It's hard to know for sure.

Persuasion moves someone from shared assumptions to a new destination. It's not dictatorial, it's reasonable. It's not preaching to the choir, it's getting to the bottom of a complex issue. It's not judging your audience's motive, it's showing the good motives they have lead to a different destination. It's not a special philosopher's club to get in, it's just a path to travel together.

So how to progress down a pathway of shared assumptions? As in, what really leads to going one way or another on a given issue, once you've got some data? The answer is **warrants,** which you probably think of as "proof."

Claims, Warrants, Impacts

A **claim** is the point you are making. Your overall point is often called your thesis, and you should notice that you will have many sub-theses along the way. For example, my general claim (thesis) may be that soccer is better than football, but I will have sub-claims along the way, like "healthier," "safer," and "more popular." In turn, any of these sub-claims may have internal sub-claims. Some debates identify that the stasis of a major issue (the overall thesis) is four or five levels deep, and everyone will focus on a particular sub-sub-sub-sub-sub claim. This is "depth." Surface-level discussions focus on claims alone, while in-depth discussions dive into the sub-claims.

You prove a claim with **warrants**. Warrants, in this case, refer to "reasons" to accept the claim. No claim should stand without reasons provided to support that claim. Reasons could include philosophy, law, statistics, maxims, personal examples, historical examples, logic, or even hearsay.

Impacts explain the function of your argument. Think of argument like an XY graph. Where the warrants prove it "true" or "likely," the impacts explain its "importance." When I coach business leaders about communications, the concept that there even is an importance scale in communication is earth shattering to many. One CEO recently blurted out "That's the problem! I have no importance scale!" She used this insight to stop overwhelming employees with emails, and think more deeply before choosing which points to argue.

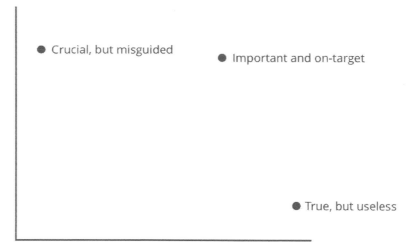

Importance

Crucial, but misguided   Important and on-target

True, but useless

Rightness / Truth

Sidenote to avoid confusion: the term "warrant" also appears in a similar context in the famous "Toulmin Model" of argumentation. The Toulmin model is more precise and fleshed out, but also more difficult to understand, as it includes Grounds, Reasons, Evidence, Warrants, Backing, Qualifiers, Rebuttals, and Claims. In debaterland and this book, "warrant" is a sort of encompassing term for grounds, reasons, evidence, and backing, while claims are associated with both claims and rebuttals. Impacts serve more of a rhetorical function than logical function, explaining how the audience should use the claims just proven with warrants.

How-To

Say this out loud: "Claims, warrants, impacts." It's the mental model for presentation of a persuasive point. Remember how to outline your talk on paper?

When speaking from the outline for your speech, you **should not** write down every claim, warrant, and impact, which is why it must become a mental habit.

Many presenters will only write down their claims, and speaking from their claims listen to themselves speak to identify the warrants, and then impact successfully because they understand the function of their argument at that time and what having proved it means (e.g. "the plan may not be trusted," "we must look to another reason, because I just refuted the standing one," or "this point outweighs all other points presented by my opponents"). So you MUST think to yourself: "when I make a point, I need a claim, I support it with warrants, and I conclude with an impact."

Below, I have extracted a short example from a team policy debate case regarding regulation of ballast water on international freight ships. See if you can identify the claims, the warrants, and the impact statements.

Problem 1: Species Lost

Biodiversity, whenever impacted, is a matter of utmost concern, as shown by kudzu raging across the south, brown tree snakes overtaking Guam, dangerous hornets in France, and so on. Biodiversity impacts set in motion serious chain reactions, the end result of which cannot even be known.

We'll prove this with an example: Viral Hemorrhagic Septicemia.
(*Source: Rebecca S. Robison [J.D. Candidate, May 2009.] "Water, Catalyst Of Life And Strife: A Threat To Security Or A Vital Opportunity To Foster Cooperation?: Comment: Bringing The Floating Polluters To Port: Why The Minnesota Pollution Control Agency Has A Nondiscretionary Duty To Regulate Ballast Water Discharge In Lake Superior And How To Avoid Impermissible Extraterritorial Effects" Hamline Law Review, Summer, 2008 [31 Hamline L. Rev. 773*])
"A new strain of an invasive virus affecting over eighteen species of fish in the Great Lakes basin has spread to all of the Great Lakes

except Lake Superior. Viral Hemorrhagic Septicemia (VHS), previously known only to Europe, Japan and the coasts of the United States, is nicknamed the 'Ebola virus' of fish because it results in internal and external hemorrhaging, bulging eyes and organ failure. Since 2003 when it was first discovered, VHS has caused massive die-offs in fish populations, threatening the Great Lakes fishing industry, valued at $ 4.5 billion annually. In a 2006 report, the United States Department of Agriculture called VHS an 'extremely serious pathogen' that 'is causing an emerging disease in the Great Lakes region.'"

Big deal you say? Just one city? Imagine this happening in every port city in the world. The potential results are a cataclysmic worst case scenario: extinction.

We turn to the Military Law Review in 1994, with Major David N. Diner LL.M
(*Source: Major David N Diner [B.S., 1980, Ohio State University; J.D., 1983; LL.M., 1993], "The Army and the Endangered Species Act: Who's Endangering Whom?," Military Law Review, Winter 1994 [143 Mil. L. Rev. 161]*)
"To accept that the snail darter, harelip sucker, or Dismal Swamp southeastern shrew could save mankind may be difficult for some. Many, if not most, species are useless to man in a direct utilitarian sense. Nonetheless, they may be critical in an indirect role, because their extirpations could affect a directly useful species negatively. In a closely interconnected ecosystem, the loss of a species affects other species dependent on it. Moreover, as the number of species decline, the effect of each new extinction on the remaining species increases dramatically. Biological Diversity. — The main premise of species preservation is that diversity is better than simplicity. As the current mass extinction has progressed, the world's biological diversity generally has decreased. This trend occurs within ecosystems by reducing the number of species, and within species by reducing the

number of individuals. Both trends carry serious future implications. Biologically diverse ecosystems are characterized by a large number of specialist species, filling narrow ecological niches. These ecosystems inherently are more stable than less diverse systems. "The more complex the ecosystem, the more successfully it can resist a stress. . . . [l]ike a net, in which each knot is connected to others by several strands, such a fabric can resist collapse better than a simple, unbranched circle of threads — which if cut anywhere breaks down as a whole." By causing widespread extinctions, humans have artificially simplified many ecosystems. As biologic simplicity increases, so does the risk of ecosystem failure. The spreading Sahara Desert in Africa, and the dustbowl conditions of the 1930s in the United States are relatively mild examples of what might be expected if this trend continues. Theoretically, each new animal or plant extinction, with all its dimly perceived and intertwined effects, could cause total ecosystem collapse and human extinction. Each new extinction increases the risk of disaster. Like a mechanic removing, one by one, the rivets from an aircraft's wings, mankind may be edging closer to the abyss.""

This problem is clearly worth solving – in many more lakes, ports, and rivers than Lake Superior alone – and so we present the following plan to address all ballast water driven environmental harm.

One fair way to analyze the argument above would be as follows:

- Claim: Marine Species Lost is a Problem
- Warrants:
    Septicemia in Lake Superior costs $4.5B / year
    The environment is interdependent and diverse
    Simplification of an ecosystem creates greater risks
    Too many ecosystems are oversimplified now

> Each one lost species risks human extinction

- Impacts:

> Environmental imbalance is dangerous
>
> This problem justifies the plan, which follows

Notice that while the warrants provide information and proves the claim, the impacts explain what to think or do now that the information has proven the claim. In other words, why did you make this point?

In cross-examination and later speeches the speaker who listened to herself read any quotations should attempt to recall and mention the precise warrants contained within those quotations.

When presenting quotations, it's key to gain the audience's attention and vocally stress the key warrants. Many presenters merely recite a quotation, and its power is lost because an audience won't really process the warrants contained within. Future explanation could be prevented by merely illuminating the words during the initial presentation.

To impact well, it is crucial to **see big picture** – how does this point relate to all the other points and potential future points? – and to understand the functions of differing argument types. For example, articulating how an argument neutralizes an opponent's argument does not "win the debate round" – it merely defeats the particular point your opponent was trying to prove with that argument. You need to analyze further whether that particular point was a "round winner" or not (usually the answer is not).

You will pick up a knack for seeing big picture by taking decent notes and learning the purpose of various types of arguments. This is why nerding out about debate and arguing with friends over how many types of significance exist is pretty helpful. When you clear up the purpose of the various arguments in your own mind you can recognize what's happening with each different argument and pick and choose which arguments need response, articulating exactly why to your audience.

The short version is that some arguments may be skipped entirely if you defeat or turn a linked argument that provides access to those arguments. There is a complete hierarchy of argument and debate could take place at any or all of the following (from the top):

- The exact words of the resolution
- Interpretation – the nature of the decision we are making today
- Weighing mechanism (value)
- Weighing mechanism (criteria)
- Facts
- Analysis and interpretation of these facts (what most people think is "debate" before they've learned about components of argument)
- Impacts – the relevance of our analysis about these facts to the decision being made
- Terminal Impacts – the final expression of harm or benefit that could occur
- A priori Impacts – impacts that come before our judgment of the substance of the round

If you don't understand ANY of the above list, that's okay! You will pick it up through the latter sections of this book and by debating. If you've debated for years and don't recognize this list, then it's time to give names to concepts you probably know, but simply haven't put to paper.

I teach a concept called "Bubbles" that helps see how this is done at a high level, but it has around 40 permutations, so you should watch the video eventually, but not until you've had at least 10 debate rounds (free on YouTube.com/ethosdebate search for Bubbles).

Claim, Warrants, and Impacts are one of the most helpful and most basic critical thinking patterns to pick up from debate. In all areas of life, it's useful to separate the point from its proof and then discuss its relevance.

Time to "Make the Case" for Something

Alright – you are ready to persuade. How exactly should you go about that? You will "make the case" for your argument.

Debaters inherited a Latin phrase from lawyer-land: *"prima facie."* It means "on its face," which really just means "on initial appearance, there seems to be a case here that is worth addressing."

For example, there is a process for serious crimes in our country where a grand jury will issue an indictment (a formal accusation of a crime). The legal standard used is "prima facie" – is there sufficient evidence available for a case against the accused. In a grand jury indictment hearing, there is no defense to present counter-evidence and say "no, they're wrong!" Only the evidence for the crime is presented. That's because the indictment is determining whether an accusation has strong enough support to demand a trial. Later, at trial, the defense will have an opportunity to answer the claims (perhaps proving innocence), and the prosecution will go much further than the initial case, in cross-examining, analyzing, and persuading.

So a "prima facie case" means enough of a case for something that, without opposition, we could in good conscience make the decision it recommends. So it's a debate starter.

One may argue that "their case is not even prima facie" when on the opposing team. It's usually a fruitless argument, since answering claims of a case may certainly defeat the case, but does not mean that the initial case lacked the merits to even consider it for a moment. Occasionally, however, you will need to articulate that a case lacked the basic components of prima facie consideration. Here are two examples:

- **Example A:** On the topic "the U.S. should reduce barriers to immigration," let's suppose an affirmative team demonstrates the top 3 problems in immigration today and sits down. The negative could successfully argue: "There is no case for a reduction in barriers, since the affirmative never articulated which barriers ought to be reduced, and did not attempt to demonstrate such a plan would work. Your consideration at this point would be premature, because no actual proposal has been articulated."

- **Example B:** On the topic "in Western Democracies, privacy ought to be valued over national security," let's suppose the first affirmative speech articulates the three key benefits of privacy, and the three worst things about national security. A savvy negative speaker could successfully argue: "There is no prima facie case for the resolution here, because no comparison was made. Simply pointing out benefits of privacy and detriments of national security does not directly compare the benefits of each to the other, or the downsides of each to the other, or really even analyze at all the comparison between the two. Isolated true statements about each term in the resolution fail to address the 'ought to be valued over' phrase in the resolution."

So what if in the next affirmative speech the speaker in Example A provides a plan, or in Example B provides a comparison? Negative should capitalize on this activity and say "by doing so, my opponents revealed that the initial case was not prima facie, and they intended to go much deeper than initially thought. This means the first speech of mine was a waste, and the debate is only now beginning, because the initial case wasn't made. In the restricted format of a debate round, there are too few remaining speeches for sufficient back-and-forth on the real case. This key admission that the initial case was not prima facie for the resolution should be the reason you vote against them. You should insist on voting on well-tested cases by the end of a debate round, which absolutely necessitates the case's existence in the first affirmative speech."

Some in debaterland will say that presentation of a prima facie case is required by the rules of debate. I disagree, but believe it is easy to articulate that a prima facie case is required by the laws of reasonability. If a team may shift their position throughout the round, then it is not reasonable to consider the position – you're still determining what the position even is!

Chapter 10. Make a Case for Something

Alright – you are ready to persuade. How exactly should you go about that? You will "make the case" for your argument. Finally!

Debaters inherited a Latin phrase from lawyer-land: *"prima facie."* It means "on its face," which really just means "on initial appearance, there seems to be a case here that is worth addressing."

For example, there is a process for serious crimes in our country where a grand jury will issue an indictment (a formal accusation of a crime). The legal standard used is "prima facie" – is there sufficient evidence available for a case against the accused. In a grand jury indictment hearing, there is no defense to present counter-evidence and say "no, they're wrong!" Only the evidence for the crime is presented. That's because the indictment is determining whether an accusation has strong enough support to demand a trial. Later, at trial, the defense will have an opportunity to answer the claims (perhaps proving innocence), and the prosecution will go much further than the initial case, in cross-examining, analyzing, and persuading.

So a "prima facie case" means enough of a case for something that, without opposition, we could in good conscience make the decision it recommends. So it's a debate starter.

One may argue that "their case is not even prima facie" when on the opposing team. It's usually a fruitless argument, since answering claims of a case may certainly defeat the case, but does not mean that the initial case lacked the merits to even consider it for a moment. Occasionally, however, you will need to articulate that a case lacked the basic components of prima facie consideration. Here are two examples:

- **Example A:** On the topic "the U.S. should reduce barriers to immigration," let's suppose an affirmative team demonstrates the top 3 problems in immigration today and sits down. The negative could successfully argue: "There is no case for a reduction in barriers, since the affirmative never articulated which barriers ought to be reduced, and did not attempt to demonstrate such a plan would work. Your consideration at this point would be premature, because no actual proposal has been articulated."

- **Example B:** On the topic "in Western Democracies, privacy ought to be valued over national security," let's suppose the first affirmative speech articulates the three key benefits of privacy, and the three worst things about national security. A savvy negative speaker could successfully argue: "There is no prima facie case for the resolution here, because no comparison was made. Simply pointing out benefits of privacy and detriments of national security does not directly compare the benefits of each to the other, or the downsides of each to the other, or really even analyze at all the comparison between the two. Isolated true statements about each term in the resolution fail to address the 'ought to be valued over' phrase in the resolution."

So what if in the next affirmative speech the speaker in Example A provides a plan, or in Example B provides a comparison? Negative should capitalize on this activity and say "by doing so, my opponents revealed that the initial case was not prima facie, and they intended to go much deeper than initially thought. This means the first speech of mine was a waste, and the debate is only now beginning, because the initial case wasn't made. In the restricted format of a debate round, there are too few remaining speeches for sufficient back-and-forth on the real case. This key admission that the initial case was not prima facie for the resolution should be the reason you vote against them. You should insist on voting on well-tested cases by the end of a debate round, which absolutely necessitates the case's existence in the first affirmative speech."

Some in debaterland will say that presentation of a prima facie case is required by the rules of debate. I disagree, but believe it is easy to articulate that a prima facie case is required by the laws of reasonability. If a team may shift their position throughout the round, then it is not reasonable to consider the position – you're still determining what the position even is!

The Goal of a Case: Structure the Entire Conversation

Here's the key point: in most of life, a "case" for something is merely a conversation starter. It's enough chips and salsa to know what's for dinner, but it's not the whole enchilada.

Only occasionally do you give a speech of some kind with zero interruption and zero followup conversation.

- **In a business meeting:** you'll make a case for something, usually called "pitching" a concept. Then folks in the room will ask questions, give alternate presentations, and you'll discuss the various points. You may still "succeed" at persuasion, but should not expect your exact original case to be adopted. Other minds and viewpoints will modify your original position. You're okay with that, because you wanted to start a reasonable movement towards the shared goal everyone has of helping customers, being profitable, or whatever is the goal.

- **In a debate round:** you'll make a case for something, but that is just the first of several speeches, and there is typically a cross-examination or other means of interaction. Over the course of the hour or so, you will hone down the reasons for your original position, perhaps modify the reasons for it slightly, and hopefully drive towards adoption of the overall resolution. Key note: in formal competitive debate, "shifting" your original position is a big no-no. But that doesn't mean you can't modify the reasons for and weight of analysis given for that original position.

- **In a conversation:** you'll make a case for something and get interrupted pretty quickly with counter-cases, opinions, questions, varying information, and so on. To persuade, you want to reach the conclusion, but it's best if your fellow conversants find their way to that conclusion on their own.

- **In most sermons:** the preacher just talks for 15–45 minutes and nobody questions the position. (This is a travesty.) It illustrates an important distinction to the young person choosing between speech and debate: in a single speech, your audience may doubt you, but it's easy to convince yourself everything went great and you know what you're talking about; in a debate, it's someone's JOB to argue against you for an hour, and you will learn to be far more disciplined in your reasoning and research and learn to adapt and think on your feet. Why? Because the conclusion you had in mind is shaped through the round. This is healthy. Preaching is one of the only forms of rhetoric besides keynote speaking where audiences get no meaningful interaction, and speakers have no way of knowing the real doubts of the audience members. How can you achieve stasis? How can you find the crux and work from it? In these formats, there is a wall of separation between the presenter and the shared assumptions of the audience.

So don't think of your "case" as your end point; it's just the beginning. Most presenters that I have worked with struggle to properly prioritize here, spending 90% of their time crafting and honing their case (or elevator pitch, slide deck, or script), neglecting to think through how they will manage and participate in the back-and-forth that happens after the case.

In reality, the case is usually less than 15% of the round. It needs to be good, but don't over-invest as if you have just one shot to persuade. You can plant seeds that don't sprout for an hour! So unlike delivery of a single speech, a case need not be perfect – it just should provide an organized structure for the conversation, with the key headlines under which the conversation will occur, and introduce the primary substance that proves the major claims.

Some Classic Case Structures

Here are a few easy structures to learn. I have committed these and a few more to memory and use them as outlines for business presentations and written documents. Note that the introduction (hook, thesis, roadmap) is common to all speeches, whether debates or presentations.

Problem-Solution

I. Introduction – Hook, thesis, roadmap
II. Key Trends – Whatever foundational facts are needed (note: no analysis of

them yet... think charts and graphs)
III. The Problem – Analysis showing how the key trends are dangerous, qualitatively or quantitatively
IV. A Proposal – Key proposal details
V. Problem Solved – Why the proposal solves the problem

Problem-Solution is the classic sales pitch: people are more easily persuaded by solutions if they feel you understand their problem well. Technically speaking, Problem-Solution is strong for gaining momentum by sharing assumptions up until point IV. Theoretically, anyone could insert a new IV and V to solve the problem you've illustrated in points II and III.

The reason so much political speech is empty rhetoric is that it consists of pointing out problems, and audiences loudly agreeing, with few workable solutions. "U.S. Immigration is a completely broken system," I say, and you nod your head. But what to do about it? Well, a politician here inserts a super vague statement that can mean anything to anyone, like "secure the border," or (my personal favorite) "we need common-sense solutions."

Don't get swindled by Problem-Solution rhetoric. It's a valuable way of thinking, but requires more time in the solutions area than many people give it. That's the weakness of this case: problem stealing. A savvy opponent may attempt to steal your momentum on the problem by contributing points to how the problem is even worse, and then present an improved alternative proposal. This is my default tactic when responding to truly important problems.

Comparative Advantage

I. Introduction – Hook, thesis, roadmap
II. Key Trends – Whatever foundational facts are needed (note: no analysis of them yet... think charts and graphs)
III. A Proposal – Key proposal details
IV. Compare/Contrast for Advantage – Demonstrate the proposal's advantage

over the current course (for each point, usually there's an A. What we're getting now, and B. What the proposal gets for us)

The Comparative Advantage is straightforward. You get to the point real quick, then spend most of your time analyzing its differences.

Use this case structure for most internal matters. If you use the Problem-Solution case when telling a potential customer about how you solve their pain, well and good. If you use Problem-Solution to pitch a new internal employee wellness initiative to your CEO, she may laser in on the problem part and feel you are discrediting her ability to lead. The solution may be great, but you'll never get there because of resistance to the problem.

It takes a certain amount of rhetorical selflessness to pitch a proposal that solves a major problem, without discussing the problem solved. Yet when it will be perceived as rubbing a problem in the face of your audience, you will alienate yourself from them and create an uphill battle. People don't have to publicly admit "I was wrong" to change, and the comparative advantage structure is a good way to give them an easy path out while saving face.

The obvious weakness of the case is that it does not build from shared assumptions. Here's this proposal, it's good. Without agreeing on the problem you're setting out to solve (we're not even mentioning problems!), your audience needs a little more help getting interested and seeing the importance of your proposal. You may need to articulate the shared assumption of how decisions are made, or gain audience identification with the concerns of your advantages.

Shared Goals

I. Introduction – Hook, thesis, roadmap
II. Existing Goals – The previously established goals of the audience, status quo, or leadership (such as a quote from the annual strategy, a law when it was passed, or a famous leader)

III. Trends Against the Goal – Foundational facts that show "we are doing something opposite of our own goals"
III. A Proposal – Key proposal details
IV. Goal Achieved – How the proposal will put things back on track to achieve the original goal

Shared Goals (sometimes called "Goals-Criteria") is my personal favorite case structure, because it works from shared assumptions in a deeper way. In Problem-Solution, we build up the Problem and hope we got it right and that the audience agrees. Our opponents (if there are any), will likely argue against the problem's significance. In Shared Goals, by identifying a real goal that already exists we work from assured common ground. There's no denying a previous goal.

Never underestimate the power of hypocrisy. If the fact pattern is trending against the goal, then hypocrisy is the result. What's beautiful is you usually do not have to say the word "hypocrisy," and can stay really positive as a presenter, but your entire audience is already thinking it: these facts appear to prove that the opposite of our goal is what we're doing. Oh no!

And then the solution, just as in Problem-Solution, is weighed for its merits in how well it achieves the goal.

To take down a Shared Goals case, most likely you will have to jettison the goal ("perhaps we should reconsider what we set out to do in the first place... times have changed"), or demonstrate that there is a higher shared goal at work here and the proposal violates that higher goal. Of course, you may argue against any weaknesses in the proof and arrangement of the case, but never underestimate the power of hypocrisy – audiences are persuaded when you put into words their logical thoughts about an issue.

Other Cases

Other case structures are usually derivatives of these three. For example, if your case is not for a proposal but merely weighing the importance of two things, you might choose comparative advantage minus a proposal. If your case is to cast blame on some idea, or show one thing unimportant, you might use the Problem-Solution structure up until the Solution part.

So can you rearrange these structures?

Of course! The structures are guidelines, and their structure may or may not be apparent to your audience during presentation. You may want to begin with the proposal, save the problem for the end, propose a new goal you think everyone really believes in despite the stated one, and so on.

My only advice is to make conscious decisions to rearrange proven patterns; don't just slop together some crazy outline because it was easier.

Should you Point Out Weaknesses in Your Own Case?

I think so. It's more reasonable. When someone acts like there are only pros to a decision and no cons, the person who says "there are both pros and cons" tends to appear more reasonable.

Admitting that your case is the **conclusion you've reached** after considering the pros and the cons actually serves to strengthen your case, not weaken it, in the eyes of most audiences. Otherwise it appears like perhaps you're paid to reach your conclusion and ignore anything else (and often, in sales, think tanks, lawyering, marketing, and analysis – you are!).

Avoiding overstatement is a key strategic lesson from debate. We'll dive into that and other strategy lessons much deeper in section two. For now, just think of this: would you rather have a discussion with an open-minded person or a close-minded person? Oh right, it's not really a discussion when there is unwillingness to consider alternative points of view. So the most persuasive people present using language that demonstrates their similarity to the audience: it was a tough choice and the other side's arguments are good, but here's why it seems to weigh out my way when all is considered.

Available Sources of Material: Think Like a District Attorney

The prosecution only uses some small percentage of available arguments and evidence. When you're preparing a case, don't think of it as "every reason I can possibly think of." A list of points is not an argument, is not a case, and shouldn't even be considered arguing. It's barely thinking...

The district attorney is going to spend forever assembling all of the research, then identifying the points of stasis, then choosing to tell a story that only includes the crucial support needed to believe the story points that lead to a verdict. Everything else is cast aside. Perhaps you will need it depending on what the opposition says, but that's not what you'll use to make the case.

A district attorney will also obsess over understanding the jury, thinking through audience backgrounds to body language, and tailor the case to that audience. A huge mistake many debaters make is to have just "one version" of their case, which is presented to every audience regardless of what they learn about the audience before the round. In college, my partner and I developed a modular case that would change every round based on the makeup of our audience – we had around eight total versions of the same core idea.

Ready to Try It?

Let's make a case! Pick an idea that you'd like to make persuasive. Now pick an audience that you'd like to persuade. Without choosing your audience first, you will inevitably fail to see things through their eyes as you construct your case.

Now get a piece of paper and a writing utensil.

Step 1: Build Logical Chain from Shared Assumption to Conclusion

Use the diagram in "shared assumptions" above for help. You'll have to identify a starting point and an end point, then build a chain between.

Step 2: Discover All Warrants for Each Logical Step (your claims)

Now write down as bullet points a simple list of every warrant you have to sway your audience at each decision point in your diagram. Remember, you can use:

- Statistics
- Laws / Precedents
- Quotations
- Maxims / Proverbs
- Personal examples
- Historical examples
- Expert testimony
- Rumors
- Logic

If an area is weak for warrants, then you may need to do some research.

Step 3: Choose Which Warrants to Feature

For each step in your logical progression, circle or highlight the one or two best warrants that will sway an audience down your path on the logical progression.

Step 4: Outline Actual Presentation (flow)

Now transfer what you've built into one of the case structures provided. While what you've built is just the argument, your full case will include introductory material, certain facts, and so on.

Step 5: Delivery

Find someone to talk to. Patiently deliver your case, watching audience cues. Avoid defensiveness, rudeness, alienation, or any other forms of "how could you possibly think otherwise?" If your audience is skeptical, do not judge their perspective – as a generally reasonable human being, their perspective is their perspective and you need to unlock how to get them to change their conclusions of their own accord.

Try varying your tone and rate of speech as you deliver.

Step 6: Listen

Get feedback and improve. Ask what your audience found least persuasive and most compelling. Do not argue with the feedback: they heard what they heard, even if it's not what you meant.

Step 7: Rewrite

Revisit your shared assumptions diagram. Did you get it right? Did your audience surprise you? Adjust accordingly and prepare your case again. Then find a new audience, and lather, rinse, repeat.

Chapter 11. Intro to Negating

Making the case for something is where an argument starts. The rest of a debate is all about responding, while making a case against.

Here's the short version

Have a thesis and case for negation. Don't whine and nitpick. After you state your negative thesis and case, respond directly to the points made by AFF in the order that they were made. Connect your arguments to your opponents by saying something like: My opponent said X, but Y is actually more accurate because Z. You will have more arguments available than you should make, so choose carefully.

Here's the semi-short version

There are a few keys to successful negating:

- **Focus on the *winning* arguments.** We call these arguments "offense." Identify why the audience should decide your way: usually some disadvantage to your opponent's way of thinking, or some idea they forgot to consider. Focus on these offensive arguments. Reductive arguments (called mitigation) lessen the power of the opposition's arguments, and should only be used when doing so strengthens your offensive arguments. Your offense carries the debate.

- **Have a case.** Tell the audience your negating thesis early, and set out to prove that thesis. Some debaters are tempted to just "go down the flow" of their opponent's argument, but that's a mistake. It gives equal weight to every argument. Instead, fully prove a thesis that completely defeats your opponents if it's considered true. Sure, they will argue against it later and you will need to win the thesis back again, but do not rest your case against your opponents without giving the judge a complete reason to vote your way.

- **Fewer arguments, in depth.** Don't try to succeed with seven arguments. Do the hard work of thinking through those seven arguments to determine which one or two are the best, then go deep to win those.

- **Don't over-explain**. Less is usually more. Too often speakers treat audiences like computers: just listen while I program you. If audiences are computers, they are less like automatons and more like AI – they think on their own. Ignite thoughts, then move on. Your audience can do some extra thinking for you and you can pick up where you left off if your opponent refutes the point.

You can come back to this summary if you're ever in a rut.

Negating Means Adapting

Debate is an adaptive activity. You already learned a variety of case structures for thinking about the first speech in the round. The next speech, presented by the negative team, will need to adapt to the first one, even if a strategy and thesis were developed before the round (a luxury, on negative!). The further the round goes, the less predictable the arguments become.

That's why great debaters learn the ins and outs of several argument types, so that they can adapt to the needs of a particular round. What types of arguments will you learn in this chapter? Glad you asked.

If debate were a martial art, your available arguments would be your weapons: nunchucks, sticks, swords, shields, ninja suits, and throwing stars. In this chapter, you'll learn six classes of offensive arguments and six classes of defensive mitigating arguments. Use defense to decrease the effectiveness of your opponent's persuasive weapons and use offense to change the audience's mind in another direction

Everything you learned in the "how to be persuasive" section applies here. You still should work from shared assumptions to lead your audience towards a different conclusion.

At the end of this chapter you should have the knowledge of a yellow belt in debate. It will be time to go out there for your belt test: successfully complete a full debate round as negative. Before exploring the available arguments, let's take a look at two important aspects of the NEG mindset.

The Negative Mindset Part 1: A Positive Thesis

What are you trying to accomplish on NEG?

As negative, it's easy to fall into a questioning or complaining mindset. Persuasive people who are against an idea, however, do much more than complain and question. They inspire us to set our sights higher and insist on something more. It's like the classic public speaking tip: end a speech on a high note, not a downer (let's try that again: ...end a speech not on a downer, but on a high note!).

As my dad would say, "don't be a nattering nabob of negativism; instead, be a pattering pabob of positivism!"

Always take a clear position. After you've heard your opponent's case, don't just throw stones and tell us it was poorly constructed. Instead, tell us what we should think about the broader question (usually the resolution). Mitigation makes their case look weaker, but your audience needs something to vote FOR – an argument that will displace your opponent's.

In a business meeting, when someone pitches an approach to a problem and we disagree with it, our "that's a bad plan" thesis would be much improved with "here's a better one," or "we've already got two initiatives tackling this problem, let's give them time to work," or "let's make an airtight decision: here are three things we would need to do before considering a plan like this."

An Isaiah story...

I remember when we learned this "have a thesis" lesson well during my second year of debate. The topic was about changing trade policies towards Africa and/or the Middle East. A popular case idea that year was to levy trade sanctions on a particular country (pre-war Iraq, Syria, Iran, and so on – this was 2002–2003).My partner and I strongly disagreed with the concept of sanctions, and would use research to show that sanctions mostly hurt poor people and solidified the power of dictators. We weren't winning with this strategy all that often. One of the problems occurred when people made a "consistency" argument, showing that the USA already has several sanctions on these countries, and AFF is making them stronger.

We had attended an economics seminar on trade,checked out several economics texts on the subject, and really felt like we had a solid position. Then someone told us "the audience needs to vote FOR something, not just

AGAINST something." And that's what flipped the switch for us. I don't think we lost another negative round against sanctions that entire year.

We looked at the power of increasing trade and how that reverses the two problems of sanctions: increasing trade can be shown to improve the economic standing of poor people and decrease the power of dictators (plus, the Pope was for it... which was a cool quote). We took a clearer position than "don't sanction Syria" or "sanctions are bad."

Our thesis was: "to get countries to change from their wicked ways, engage, don't isolate." This repackaged the same arguments in a far more effective way because we had a positive thesis.

The Negative Mindset Part 2: Reasonable Doubter

We wanted to title this part "Doubting Thomas," but everyone is mildly annoyed by that personality. Rather than the "you'd have to hit me with a brick in the face to prove it exists" persona, you want to portray the "I'd like to agree, but can't quite yet" reasonable persona.

So yes, you'll refute. Yes, you'll doubt. Yes, you'll say your opponents did not meet the burden of proof. But no, you won't say "nuh-uh" to every single point they make.

With that said, you should take a skeptic's mindset into a debate round. We all know an iceberg is deceptive because it has a portion that we see and then a several times larger portion that we do not. The skeptic says "hey AFF, I think you may be at the limits of your knowledge on that last argument... it looks like an iceberg, but it's really just a plastic mountain painted white."

I cannot tell you how often I end up asking novice and intermediate debaters "so, what you're saying is that you took them at their word?" "Well... yeah. They were so reasonable!" I usually hear in reply. Ok... so they acted like they were persuaded by their own position. That doesn't mean you have to act the same way.

How do you doubt well? Don't look at what they said, look at what they didn't say. Spot what's missing. A phrase that should habitually be running through your head is "in order to agree with this point, you'd have to believe ___," and then fill in the blank. I actually use this and constantly generate material that no one has mentioned yet.

Here's an example. AFF says that their plan for space-based solar power has all kinds of research backing it, and can work if we would just fund the plan. It's as simple as putting solar panels on satellites. Now as NEG, we can try and argue against solar panels or satellites as stable methods for space-based solar power, but we're probably going to get wrecked by scientific research. That's what AFF is saying.

What have they not said, based on the above example?

- That it's secure – Space debris or terrorist/enemy rockets might easily take out our unsecured, free-floating power sources.
  How it gets to earth – Are we talking battery cell transportation through a constant stream of rockets? Beams that may be intercepted? No doubt the power can be collected, but then what?
- That the Government should do this – Governments are great at investing in yesterday's technology for tomorrow's challenge (insert F−22 example... but I digress). This seems like something that Elon Musk, Tesla, Google, or Amazon should be coming up with, not the Government. That the Government is behind so much of our infrastructure is already a big enough problem.
- That it's really more efficient than other stuff being researched – We're researching power initiatives to harness the waves, wind, and more... right here on earth.

These are just some clues to get us started on reasonable doubters. Our research and arguments against this case should go further, but let's get off on the right foot by not believing that AFF is revealing the complete story.

Available Arguments – A Negating Arsenal

In Chapter 2 of *Rhetoric*, by Aristotle, he defines rhetoric as follows: "the faculty of observing in any given situation the available means of persuasion." Without getting too deep, he's saying that rhetoric is about thinking habits (a faculty) that rapidly identify (observation in a given situation) what exists that's useful for persuading (the available means of persuasion). The faculty comes with practice, the observation comes with strategy and a variety of given situations, but the available means of persuasion are pretty well defined.

Classical Rhetoric provides a list of available means of persuasion for all situations called the "common topics" (topics that are common to any discourse), each with its own sub-topics, and then a list of special topics for the different predominant modes of discourse (deliberation, judgement, and ceremony). From this rich tradition, we arrive at a few topics common to debate that you should know. But think of these as the "topic" level – each has myriad subtopics, which we cover in Section 2, the next volume of this book series.

Your primary available arguments are separated into two classes: Offense and Mitigation. The following two chapters will explain and exemplify each of these 12 tools.

Your primary macro-refutation tools for **Offense**:

> 1. **Disadvantages and Consequences** – Reveal a problem created by your opponent's plan or way of thinking.
> 2. **Counterplan + Disadvantages** – Show an alternative approach to

the same issue that does not have the disadvantage of your opponent's plan.

3. **Deeper Principles** – Demonstrate that some more important idea is at stake and excludes your opponent's position.

4. **Outweighing Contention** – Overcome your opponent's position on the shared assumption of some common goal or value – literally show "it's the opposite that's true."

5. **Topicality/Resolutionality** – Demonstrate your opponents are off-topic and should not be heard.

6. **Procedurals and Kritiks** – Show that your opponents have committed some offense to process or propriety and should not be heard.

Your options for micro-refutation are nearly unlimited, because who knows what your opponents will say and how they will say it? Your job is to put words to doubts.

Your primary micro-refutation tools for **Mitigation**:

1. **Logical Gaps** – Respond to the *Reasoning*

2. **Methodological Flaws** – Respond *to the Research*

3. **Alternative Data** – Respond with *Counter Research*

4. **Significance** – Respond to the *Importance*

5. **Causal Analysis** – Respond to the *Deeper Why*

6. **Predictive Analysis** – Respond to the *Solution*

How should you balance these arguments? We want to say "it's situational," but that's a frustrating answer for beginners. We recommend about 2/3 of your arguments as macro-refutation and about 1/3 as micro-refutation, but learning to use judgment is one of the benefits of debating. Each situation is different, so you learn all these tools for the various life situations you'll encounter.

Did we mention that all of these strategies work in real life? That's why we're teaching them here. If you want to start noticing, try and categorize things you say in a given day as a case for something, macro-refutation, or micro-refutation. Just like learning to type, you'll soon habitually think of your responses by different names.

And then it will come in handy. You'll be in a conversation and realize you could make several micro-refutation points, but will seem nitpicky, so you opt for a counterplan, since offense wins points anyways.

Last, but not least, don't forget the audience's perspective. They're far less interested in hearing someone complain about someone else's arguments. Instead, have your own thesis and then compare/contrast. If it helps, think of yourself as AFF even when you're NEG – you've got a case, not just some arguments against your opponents. Then your debating will take on a more positive tone. Instead of persuading us against something, you'll persuade us for something else. Now that's some upside down debating!

Let's build your negative toolkit.

Chapter 12. Negating – Offense/Macro-Refutation

Offensive arguments are often called positions, which is one of the definitions of "thesis." Each of these can become a speech in itself, or at least a position with several sub-points. That's why they are macro (high-level) forms of refutation: they refute entire ideas, not just the pieces of ideas (see Mitigation, below).

1. Disadvantages and Consequences

Disadvantages are the cornerstone of negative strategy. If you can successfully demonstrate that the proposed idea leads to results that just aren't worth it, then you're almost always going to persuade your audience.

The key question is: what is most worthwhile? For example, let's say AFF has proposed the Government's national institutions of health research pursue promising, life-saving cancer research, and hire the best and brightest. What are some available disadvantages?

One disadvantage is the "bottomless hole" of financial costs, another is that "government involvement in science limits innovation rather than expanding

158

it." The first disadvantage will result in a lives-vs-money debate, where what is worthwhile doesn't favor your side. There's extra work to do. The second disadvantage, however, will ultimately result in the argument that lives are more likely saved through existing private sector approaches and not the government. "At most," NEG should say, "the Government should merely provide some incentive for solving the problem, but never get involved in the actual innovation phase."

The second disadvantage impacts to something clearly worthwhile: lives saved. It creates a debate centered on this crux: when it comes to saving lives (shared assumption of worth), should the Government be patient and let the private sector arrive at cures to disease, or get involved? Now that's a good debate.

What about questions of value? Meet your new friend, the Consequence. It's the same thing as a disadvantage but used when your opponent has not proposed a specific plan. Instead, you will test some likely consequences of your opponent's philosophy and ask your audience to reject the philosophy because its consequences are unacceptable.

An Isaiah story...

For example, I once debated negative against the topic "Resolved: that U.S. Foreign Policy inappropriately emphasizes military action over diplomacy." The consequence was my favorite argument. Here are two I used regularly:

1. End Humanitarian Missions – In this consequence, I argued that the AFF idea would preclude use of the military for peacekeeping missions. Some specific ones include fighting piracy and keeping global shipping safe, humanitarian operations, and nation-building. As negative, I argued that the AFF way of thinking would preclude these activities, which in the end are better than the words of diplomacy. Lives are saved, and the world is able to do commerce because of these military actions.

2. No NATO – In this consequence, I argued that the concept of the North Atlantic Treaty Organization (NATO) would never have existed and Russia

would have won over all of Europe during the Cold War. Ultimately, NATO's Article 5 (the clause that an attack on one is an attack on all) was an expression of military action that resulted in peace. Lives were saved, and an enemy was defeated because of NATO.Here we are testing the strength of AFF's resolve by seeing if they would be willing to get rid of NATO and humanitarian missions. If their idea would lead to that conclusion, most judges would rapidly sign a negative ballot because of the apparent good of such military actions.

To structure a disadvantage is pretty simple. You just need to show a **cause** and an **effect.** (You will find more advanced disadvantage structures in Section 2... if and when we publish that thing!)The cause should be AFF's thinking, AFF's rhetoric, or AFF's specific plan. The effect should be an analysis of why AFF ends up with more harm than benefit. You may use the word "link" for cause and "impact" for effect and you'll sound like a smart debater... but for most audiences I recommend just going with good old "cause" and "effect."

Disadvantages are your core offense. The next type of offense is based on a disadvantage, but takes it a step further.

2. Counterplan + Disadvantages

One of the most persuasive things an AFF can do is create a sense of fear or danger by illustrating problems. Solving problems is much more difficult, but audiences are willing to feel "at least I'm doing something" emotions to chip away at the problem. This is where the counterplan comes in.

Why not use the presented problem as the shared assumption between AFF and NEG? Remember that persuasion works from shared assumptions. So if all in the room can agree on the problem, the debate can become a debate about which solution has the least disadvantage and highest chance of success.

Arguing that the problem is real, but AFF's solution is poor is the first half of this argument. You complete the strategy by explaining the type of solution that would be effective as you compare your solution to AFF's solution. The basis of that comparison is a disadvantage, but now the disadvantage is comparing and contrasting to the NEG solution. That sounds complicated, but it's not. Here is an example...

One year the topic was about changing U.S. policy towards India. One AFF demonstrated the problem of baby trafficking: people kidnap or sell their babies to horrible orphanages in India that try to get these babies adopted overseas, charging around $9,000–13,000 in the process (the same as a lawyer made annually in India at the time – so good money).

The AFF plan was to cap the amount an American can pay in a transaction to adopt a baby from India. NEG should never argue that kidnapping babies is okay, especially since AFF can show that an orphanage needs to sell 5 babies in a year and can lose 95 to do well. Instead, NEG should agree that the baby trafficking problem is real and argue that it's even larger than AFF said: babies are trafficked to more countries than the USA, and from more countries than India.

NEG should continue by arguing that an international problem warrants an international solution, and anything less guarantees the root problem will continue to grow while the U.S. turns a blind eye. The NEG proposes an alternative solution to the same problem. But notice that the debate round must be won by the disadvantage of doing AFF's plan instead of NEG's plan: a partial solution that masks the root issue and makes it worse. This disadvantage is what will win the round, but it needed a counterplan to even materialize as a disadvantage.

Let's look at a few more examples of the counterplan and disadvantage:

> 1. On the topic: "National security ought to be valued above freedom of the press" many AFFs would point out that today's terrorist has

unparalleled speed and that enemies are interconnected and more dangerous than ever before. Clearly a problem. The puzzle was how can NEG redirect the fear of enemies towards the "freedom of the press" side of the resolution? One way is to argue that national security should be defensive only, and not so spread out over the world threatening everyone to want to come and blow us up in the first place Freedom of the press helps keep government in check, and increasing it would reduce overall government actions in the first place... the main cause of anti-U.S. terrorism.

2. Early in this chapter we wrote about trade policies that increase sanctions. Usually AFFs arguing for sanctions would rest their case on the problem: Syrian human rights violations, Egyptian totalitarianism, Iranian state support of terrorism, and so on. For our "engage, don't isolate" strategy to work, we had to agree that the problem is real, and redirect its persuasive power: "If you want to see human rights improve in Syria, then pursue increased trade with them instead of isolating them." Our disadvantage was that sanctions would just make the problem worse as regimes blame the U.S. for their own poverty, while trade creates exchange, friendships, and wealth from the bottom up that will ultimately topple the totalitarian power of an evil regime and provide incentive not to support terrorism against the country that is feeding you.

3. On the topic: "That governments have a moral obligation to assist other nations in need," obviously AFFs show the global problems of nations in need. How could NEG redirect that shared assumption of the problem to non-assistance? One way would be to argue for long-term self-sufficiency of these nations. NEG can argue that the disadvantage of helping is that it creates a dependency, but pursuing

programs that "teach a man to fish" rather than passing out handouts is a more stable, long-term solution. If NEG can prove this disadvantage and offer a viable alternative, NEG has a powerful offensive argument.

The counterplan is a powerful argument that works persuasively by sharing the assumption with your opponents that the problem is real. But remember that the counterplan merely creates new space for a disadvantage, but the disadvantage is what ultimately persuades the audience.

3. Deeper Principles

Another form of offense is to cut your opponents off at the knees with a deeper shared assumption that excludes the initial AFF arguments. This deeper assumption may be called a goal, an objective, a criterion, a weighing mechanism, or a value. By seeing deeper, you can show that AFF's tempting arguments crossed a line by violating a principle.

This approach can be challenging because it usually requires an entire "case" as NEG. When arguing for a deeper value, you not only exclude your opponent's arguments, but include your own. It is these arguments that ultimately win the debate round. Let's take a look...

Consider this topic: "In formal education liberal arts ought to be valued above practical skills." Debate coaches obviously think this resolution is true, since we teach a liberal art! An AFF is going to argue that liberal arts increase the wisdom of society, help people find purpose and meaning, show the deeper why to life, make better leaders, lead to innovators, and prevent decay of society to utilitarianism.

So let's put our NEG hat on: liberal arts do all of those things, so it's going to be tough to argue against that part of the argument. But debate is about learning to break a large problem into its pieces and analyze those pieces – this is critical thinking. So what if we argue that "gainful employment" is the goal of formal education, while wisdom and meaning are goals of family, religion, and private life? Now we're not arguing against our conviction that liberal arts are more valuable, but we're excluding the relevancy of those arguments from the round by showing that formal education should not be about those things.

We've countered with a goal of formal education: gainful employment. This excludes rather than refutes our opponent's case. So far, so good. But to actually win the debate round we need to prove our point, with support for our own side: how practical skills emphasis in formal education leads to gainful employment. So we're going to make that point as our primary contention, right after we've persuaded the audience to the counter-goal of gainful employment.

This offensive argument has three parts:

> 1. **Value** – The counter goal/value/objective/criterion itself. Usually you should name it, define it, and supply the reasons for its superiority as the deeper principle. Spend 45 to 90 seconds explaining this value.
> 2. **Exclusion** – Argue which arguments of AFF are excluded. Not because AFF was "wrong" about them, but because the deeper principle excludes their truthfulness from mattering. The importance scale is at work! Go line by line through the AFF case for 30–45 seconds showing which points no longer count.
> 3. **Fulfillment** – Show that the deeper goal is supported by your side of the resolution. You should probably provide some logical argument backed by examples, statistics, and/or quotations. Budget 45 seconds to 4 minutes.

As you can see, it really is a "case" against your opponents. Let's consider some examples.

One topic was: "Developing countries ought to prioritize economic growth over environmental protection." An AFF may argue that the people of a nation need to first get out of poverty before they consider anything else, regardless of the consequences. The goal of AFF seems to be "getting out of poverty." What if "long-term sustenance" of the earth is a more important principle? That's a NEG strategy that could exclude AFF arguments, even though they are right that economic development likely brings people out of poverty.

Another topic was "Walmart's business practices are detrimental to the United States." One AFF team had a case focusing on how Walmart creates heavy pressures on suppliers to lower prices, which cause shortcuts or incredibly low profit rates. A team I watched found this case pretty easy to beat by actually turning that fact into an advantage by arguing for a deeper principle: benefit consumers. NEG argued that the way to determine if a business practice is detrimental or not is tied up in its impact on end-customers, nothing else. They then excluded AFF arguments, showing that those suppliers are producers, not consumers. Finally, they showed that by Walmart demanding efficiency, it creates efficiencies that lower prices for consumers. AFF should have taken an approach less susceptible to argument from economic principle.

An Isaiah story...

One parli resolution I debated in college was: "Invade North Korea." The GOV team (AFF) showed what great evils happen in North Korea, and how they're a threat to the rest of the world. They argued that the USA should lead an invasion and that it would likely succeed.

The OPP strategy that we prepped worked beautifully to exclude all of these points. We argued that Just War Theory should be the criteria by which the USA determines whether it engages in a conflict, showing the historical development of this theory through St. Augustine and St. Thomas Aquinas, among others.

1. **Value** – We convinced the judge that Just War Theory was the way to judge the moral ability to go to war.

2. **Exclusion** – We showed that being a threat to the rest of the world and the domestic injustices committed by North Korea may be true, but don't apply to any prongs of Just War Theory.

3. **Fulfillment** – Then we showed that the war on North Korea fails to meet the Right Authority and Last Resort prongs of Just War Theory, whereas keeping our peace fulfills the theory. So we had one contention on Right Authority and one contention on Last Resort.

4. Outweighing Contention

If you understood the deeper principle argument, then this argument should seem simple. Instead of proposing a new deep principle and showing that your side of the resolution meets that principle, appeal to the same principle as your opponent and show that your side meets it better.

If this offensive strategy seems straightforward, that's because it is. Unlike the last argument, you don't need to provide a new value (though you may need to clarify assumed principles), you don't exclude your opponent's arguments on the basis of another principle, but you do that last bit of building an alternative view through example, quotation, statistics, and so on.

One of the most common approaches to this argument is to try and out long-term your opponent.

1. Your opponent values national security, so you show that your

opponent's case gets short-term national security, but undermines long-term national security. For example, if their case unilaterally invaded some country, you've argued that NATO or some alliance should do the same thing.

2. Your opponent shows how one method of education leads to a better society, and you show that generationally another method leads to a better society... better.

3. Your opponent provides assistance to trafficked babies from India to the USA, you provide a more complete solution for all trafficked babies globally, no matter where they go.

This argument may be considered a brute force argument, but it's also a "seeing more deeply" argument because you work from the same shared assumption as your opponent.

5. Topicality/Resolutionality

Welcome to debaterland. This is the part of the show where we get technical. But fear not, what you're about to learn makes sense in the real world as well.

Imagine a business conference on marketing. In the breakout rooms there are 20 talks to choose from, and you have a tough decision... see your favorite author speak, or learn more about email marketing, which is the primary reason you came to the conference. Frustrated that your favorite author is two rooms down and you could have met her, you attend the "50 email marketing hacks to grow your business" talk.

You take a front row seat so you can ask questions. The room fills up to standing room only on the edges, with probably 350 people there. The speaker starts. It takes about four minutes until your suspicions are confirmed: the speaker used a great headline to get a huge audience, but is not going to deliver as promised.

Instead, this speaker is giving a talk on how to email market to people aged 55–75. Your company doesn't even sell anything to that demographic.

You just want to leave the room. But you are up in front and it would be super rude to leave, so you suffer through the next hour of how to email the aging and bolt out of the room to try and meet your author. She's gone.

"What a waste of time!" you say, and go buy yourself an extra large coffee milkshake beverage thing the barista called an iced latte. Half your day was ruined because the speaker was off-topic.

Somewhere Scott Berkun (author of *Confessions of a Public Speaker*) felt an imbalance in the force, like a collective 350 hours of productivity were just snuffed out of existence. Scott offers this math to professional speakers: take the average hourly rate of your audience (maybe $65 at a marketing conference) and multiply it by the audience (350 in this example) and realize that if you waste that hour you've just wasted $22,000 in opportunity cost.

Does that story sound painfully true? Yeah, it is. Happened to us... more than once.

When topics are printed on paper, society has a pretty general unspoken rule: the speaker should fulfill the promise of that topic. Imagine a Supreme Court case on the topic of warrantless surveillance using drones where the first lawyer to speak creatively discusses drones as remote-controlled devices, and talks about drones submerged and on land when the real question has to do with aerial surveillance. The Justices are going to get that lawyer on track or out of the court. Or if a chiropractor posed as a general physical therapist and started treating all forms of sports injuries... the discipline to stay on topic can have ranging impacts across law, medicine, ethics, and academia.

The very definition of debate includes the concept of agreeing upon a topic. It's a disciplined notion of helping an audience make an informed decision on a specified matter of controversy. When debaters veer from the topic to debate something unexpected, the negative team experiences similar emotions to our frustrated conference attender above.

But sometimes it's more subtle. In debate, you may have spent months preparing for your debate and missing the topic by a single word may change everything. Here are a few example resolutions, with some ways that the on-topic/off-topic nature of arguments affected the debate:

"Resolved: When in conflict, the right to individual privacy is more important than national security."

- A case that argues about privacy in general, rather than the "right" to privacy would not precisely prove the resolution.
- Some argued that widespread surveillance, like phone monitoring, was not relevant to the topic, since those are "collective privacy" not "individual privacy" issues.
- Some debaters drew a line between homeland security (internal) and national security (external) to exclude examples like TSA airport scanners.

"Resolved: In formal education liberal arts ought to be valued above practical skills."

- Many debates centered on whether examples were truly "formal education" examples, in formats like internships, apprenticeships, and residencies.
- "Classical liberal arts" and "liberal arts" don't mean the same thing – liberal arts is broader.
- Not all practical skills are the type of practical skills one learns in a formal education environment.

"Resolved: The United States federal government should substantially reform its trade policy with one or more of the following nations: China, Japan, South Korea, Taiwan."

- Trade sanctions are not actually trade policy, since they aren't administered by the U.S. Trade Representative and are levied for national security reasons, not economic ones.
- Reform can only include unilateral action like trade proposals, not "agreements" between the U.S. and one of the countries, since the resolution only asks the U.S. to change policy.
- Plans that provide benefits or exceptions to certain businesses inside of one of the foreign nations are not actually trade policy with the nation, but instead with the company.

In all of the examples above, there is room for disagreement on what the two sides even showed up to debate. Most audiences are willing to give a slight amount of leniency, understanding that terms can mean different things to different people, but you may find yourself in need of making an "off-topic" accusation and have to persuade the judge about the meanings of words.

To format a topicality argument, you will need the following parts:

1. **Alternative Interpretation:** What you argue the words and phrases really mean. This is your position on the correct way to view the resolution. Interpretations may be short or long: "trade sanctions are not trade policy," or "the individual right to privacy only concerns privacy violations where the individual is specifically named and targeted, not generally

probed like through the same metal detector as everyone else."

2. **Reasons to Prefer:** Your reasons to prefer may include definitions, expert quotations, contextual usages of the phrase in question, historical etymology of the phrase, and more. The key is to spend some time proving the merits of your interpretation.

3. **Reasons to Negate:** Your similar reasons to reject your opponent's apparent interpretation. You may use standards here, which are general principles about what makes an interpretation better or worse. For example, you may argue that when debating U.S. policy, "how policymakers use the phrase" is a better way to interpret the resolution than a dictionary definition.

4. **Impact:** Why the interpretation matters. Common reasons include an appeal to the rules or common sense, or arguing that impacts of interpretations won't be debated as deeply as they deserve because off-topic debates test the research sneak-attack rather than merits of arguments. For example, defining foreign policy to include private actions taken by citizens of one country toward another country (such as freezing bank accounts of individuals in China who abuse human rights) distorts the resolution to an overly broad scale. This can sound like complaining or playing the victim to an audience, which is one of the touchy parts of topicality. The key is to avoid complaining, but instead genuinely stand for reasonable and helpful debates.

These four are the general subparts of a topicality argument, but these subparts do not have to be presented in that format. We recommend the "ideal versus actual" format when you first start debating. Prove what "ideally" should have happened, then show what "actually" happened. Interpretation and reasons to prefer will fit into your explanation of the ideal, while reasons to negate and impact will fit under the actual side.

When running topicality, make sure you realize what you're asking for: *you are saying even if my opponent's actual arguments are right, you should vote against them for being off-topic.* That's hard to sell: you're asking to win even if you lose. But if you sell it, it wins the entire debate round.

Life lesson here... if you're in a business meeting and think that whoever is speaking is way off the topic of the meeting, you could make a similar argument: we're here to make a different decision, and so our decision on this issue is going to be poor since we didn't come prepared to discuss it. Making that point, however, requires incredible finesse... you're asking for someone who is making decent points to cease speaking. Don't be surprised if they take it personally. Perhaps it's better to hold the tongue now and then, or practice debate rounds so you can learn to sell this without appearing antagonistic.

An Isaiah story...

> As a novice 15-year old debater, I thought topicality was awesome. 15-year old dudes typically love black and white technicalities – it feels like a rule.At our first major tournament ever, my partner and I were up against the most senior team there. It was a certain loss for us.
>
> The topic was that the U.S. should significantly change its agriculture policy (2001–2002). We had researched the U.S. Code and found that there was a section of the U.S. Code (Title 7)

titled "Agriculture." It's like there was a specific list of agriculture policies, with around 115 total items, ranging from honeybees to hemp.

Our opponent's mother watched in horror as we latched onto one argument against her sons' really tough-to-beat case. We were terrible speakers, but found one nugget of gold: their case on wetlands wasn't in Title 7, which in our view was the most reasonable definition of U.S. agriculture policy.

We convinced the judge of our interpretation, and the judge voted for us on this technicality.

Glory! Or not... that mother became our enemy. It would've been better to have lost, from a "rest of our lives" perspective.

Yes, debate mirrors real life.

6. Procedurals and Kritiks

Procedurals argue that some process relevant to the nature of the forum has been violated. Kritiks argue that some fundamental assumption is flawed, even if the case is okay in general. In both cases the NEG argues that either the process violation or the flawed assumption is serious enough to warrant a vote against the AFF.

In family politics, a procedural would be "you can't talk yet, because Grandma hasn't finished playing the Christmas song." A Kritik would be "you watch that tone of voice, young man! Your lack respect for your elders is wrong and you must go out there with the youngsters." In both cases, the content of what you were going to say might have been perfectly fine, but it either came at the wrong time or violated some fundamental belief precluding your right to speak in the first place.

In a business where the CEO is stepping down, a procedural would be that the CEO authorized some deal far beyond his legal authority granted by the board of directors. A Kritik would be the CEO had a scandalous affair with an intern. Neither necessarily mean the CEO is doing a poor job helping the company be profitable, but both are serious objections to keeping the CEO around.

Just like topicality, procedurals and kritiks do not counter the substance your opponent's case directly. Instead, these arguments point to the violation of some process or an outright offense as the basis to reject their case. Be forewarned: these arguments can make lifelong enemies, because they can get personal.

There is not an exhaustive list of available procedurals and kritiks. Technically, topicality is a procedural: you're arguing that the procedure of staying on topic was not followed. Take a look at these other examples and you'll get the idea.

Procedural: opponents went over time. It can be easy to make a mistake, but debate is governed by strict rules and you should vote against them for having more speaking time. (note: debaters will often forfeit the round if they discover they caused this mistake)

- Procedural: opponents brought up a new argument in rebuttals. That doesn't mean vote against them, but it does mean you have to discount and ignore that argument, since rebuttals are for analyzing issues already on the table.

- Procedural: opponents do not have full text of their plan. Perhaps your opponents are passing a small bill in Congress and when you asked questions about the plan, they dodged them in CX or seemed to arbitrarily say the policy does or doesn't do certain things. That makes it difficult to claim disadvantages, since they may merely turn around and say "oh, there's an exception in our policy that prevents the disadvantage." And THEN when you asked for the full text of the bill they were passing, they didn't have it. So you're debating a moving target.

- Procedural: misrepresenting evidence. Perhaps your opponents quoted from an article, but quoted the section where an author says "some say..." right before refuting what people say. Only, your opponents left out the "some say" part and pretended the author said what the author was about to refute. This type of thing should be brought to tournament directors in a debate round, but sometimes must be addressed in round (or, outside of debate, in a meeting or around a conference table). In business, this can get you fired (and in debate, expelled from a tournament), so recognize that such claims are serious procedural accusations. It is usually wiser to ask some questions and dig deeper in the round, then make any points you need to later in rebuttals.

- Kritik: classified information. Suppose that in a foreign policy topic, your opponents have argued a side that could only be refuted by Government information that is classified. Your strategy may become arguing that classified information is key to the decision, so you can't really debate the case, but it should be rejected anyhow on the basis that the case is legally non-debatable.

- Kritik: offensive language. Gendered language or swearing kritiks occasionally come up, where you ask the audience to reject your opponent for words or phrases they have said that are offensive or flippant towards tragedy. In debate leagues where general audiences are judges, the frequency of such arguments is extremely low. One example was a kritik against quotations that had racial slurs against Hispanics, used during an immigration debate.

- Kritik: threat construction. Your opponent's language and advocacy propagate the idea that governments must respond to and monitor threats. But these threats rarely pan out. Arguing policy on the basis of perceived threats just ends up with our soldiers needlessly dying, and sparking a cycle of short term military reactions that empower government.

- Kritik: dehumanizing language. Your opponent is debating about education and keeps using language that treats graduating successively higher levels of education as "success." Their policy aims to make "more people successful, by increasing the college graduation rate." You argue that this type of thinking makes those with lesser education somehow less valuable in our eyes, as humans, like they should regret something in their life. This kritik may be extended by arguing that such thinking turns economic worth into the only measure of human worth.

The procedural format is the same as Topicality. You can keep the ideal versus actual structure, or expand to the full alternative interpretation, reasons to prefer, reasons to negate, and impact. Or learn and adopt some other tactic! Some people like interpretation, standards, violation, and impact.

Some will also break out the "alternative interpretation" into "alternative" and "interpretation," where interpretation is merely your thesis and alternative articulates what your opponents should have done. Don't overthink this... it's just multiple ways of saying the same thing: to prove that something wrong happened you must be able to articulate that there was some way not to commit that wrong. If you are going to chide your opponents for using certain language, be sure to provide a reasonable alternative ("they could have just said 'visa-overstayers,' but they said 'heinous criminals,' etc.") But be sure you are being reasonable as well. If NEG argues that saying the phrase "illegal immigrant" is dehumanizing, but the debate topic itself contained the phrase, then there was no real way to avoid this as the AFF team. It's difficult to convince a judge to vote against a team when the supposedly problematic phrase was in the actual resolution. It is impossible for them to debate this topic without using the phrase, so choose a different argument.

Since procedurals and kritiks ask for rejection of your opponents even if their argument was otherwise sound, you must understand the shift that happened: you asked your audience to reject your opponents themselves, not their arguments. That's why it feels personal. It is.

Yet, sometimes you must be prepared to debate about the debate, rather than the substance of the debate. Procedurals and kritiks are how you debate about the debate.

Macro-refutation is powerful. It's where the "negative case" comes from. Now let's look at macro-refutation's best friend: micro-refutation.

Chapter 13. Negating – Mitigation/Micro-Refutation

Where offense helped us persuade our audience to our side, Mitigation helps us reduce the persuasion of our opponent. Think of it like a number line. +1 is your opponent's side of the resolution, 0 is neutral, and -1 is your side. When negating, mitigation arguments take that +1 and get it closer to 0 (or maybe all the way there!). But you could have a -2 disadvantage that moves us all the way t to -3 on the negative side of the line..

Blah blah numbers. There is no exhaustive list of your available mitigating arguments. This book doesn't aim to teach you all of the arguments either, because they come from the rest of your education: history, logic, statistics, research, civics, and so on. Debate is an integrative subject, bringing in what you learned from other subjects and deploying them.

Unlike our offensive argumentation discussed above, you can think of mitigation as "responses" to your opponents. Here are a few classes of responses:

1. Logical Gaps – Respond to the *Reasoning*

There are myriad ways to refute that the conclusions drawn by your opponents were reasonable. You may occasionally argue that their logic did not follow at all, but more likely will show that their conclusions were somewhat overstated. Your goal here is to diminish the power of their argument so that your macro-refutation is even more persuasive – you don't have to "defeat" their argument.

There are two primary classes of logical gaps: structural flaws (meaning the argument missed some core building block) and logical fallacies (meaning the argument did not rationally identify the appropriate conclusion). One of my favorite things to do is think through the requirements of arguments – like the four parts of topicality in the offense section – and expose the importance of any missing piece. That's why you want to learn and think about the parts of arguments, so that you can recognize when one part is missing.

Here are a few example responses in action, as you might present the arguments live:

> 1. **Appeal to Extremes:** My opponents have used the Japanese Internment Camps example as if it is a representative action of what our Government does when it comes to privacy and security. But having to reach back seven decades to find a representative example should tell you something, and that Ronald Reagan later apologized for the Government should tell you something else. Look to arguments that represent common Government actions, not extremes, as the reason to consider my opponent's ideas.
>
> 2. **Alternate Causes:** My opponents have acted like the cause of Iranian poverty is U.S. sanctions and read a quotation that says sanctions increase poverty. But that does not mean sanctions are the sole reason for poverty in Iran – or even a significant factor. You need

to see an analysis of all factors leading to poverty – economic, governmental, and external – before drawing the conclusion that sanctions are a major contributor.

3. **Failed Proof / Red Herring:** My opponents told you everything great about national security, but this debate is about choosing between national security and the individual right to privacy when they clash. Just because national security is good (privacy is too!) doesn't mean it should be prioritized over privacy. By neglecting to contrast privacy in the exact scenarios my opponent has mentioned national security, the core question has been neglected entirely.

4. **Underdeveloped Solution:** My opponent spent eighty percent of his speaking time discussing the problems with our immigration system. That's the one thing both sides agree on, and everyone from politicians to Panamanians. The issue isn't whether or not the immigration system is broken, but which way to go to fix the problem: more openness or more enforcement. Focus the rest of the round on whether his solution is advantageous, out of available solutions – not on whether it attempts to address a real problem.

5. **No Counter-definition:** My opponent argued that my case is not topical, saying our definition of "medical malpractice" was problematic. Let's say that it is for a second... now what? My opponent failed to provide a definition that works, so even if mine is flawed, it's all you have to go with! Don't vote on complaints against an interpretation if there is no satisfactory counter-interpretation.

6. **Appeal to Lack of Evidence:** My opponent said "no one has proven that this life-saving drug is unsafe," but this is nothing short of burden shifting. It takes 7–14 years for most clinical studies to determine the safety of a drug. That's why the burden is to prove the

drug is safe before allowing it to be used in hospitals, not the other way around. No one dying from this drug, yet, does not lead us to conclude it is safe.

7. **No Causal Link:** My opponent has claimed that my plan to help Taiwan with trade will somehow result in China declaring war. But they tied together two different authors to say that trade upsets China and that upsetting China can lead to war – neither author would think our plan actually leads to war, because they mean that little word "upset" in completely different ways to completely different degrees. My plan does not cause war with China.

As you can see, all that logic you learned is valuable. Just be forewarned that the "THAT'S A FALLACY" speaker is usually a major turn-off. Rather than naming fallacies, explain the substance of what's wrong – why certain premises don't lead to their conclusions.

2. Methodological Flaws – Respond *to the Research*

Another class of responses has to do with questioning the support offered by your opponents. While it varies by nature of the debate topic, often studies are used to assist in proving arguments. Every way a study can go wrong is an available response. Here are a few examples:

1. **Cherry-picked Sample:** My opponent is claiming that people are willing to pay higher taxes for more medical benefits, but the poll was a random daytime calling poll. You're only going to get retired people by calling at that time! The sample cares far more about healthcare than the normal population and is non-representative.

2. **False Cause:** While true that Washington D.C.'s crime since the gun ban in 1970 went up dramatically over the next 40 years, it fails to account for the dramatic increase in gang violence and violence caused by the war on drugs. When you look at just the statistics since 1990 when D.C. augmented its police force to national averages, crime actually went down under the gun ban. The gun ban isn't the cause of increasing or decreasing crime in D.C.

3. **No Methodology:** My opponent has relied on a so-called study by the Heritage Foundation that claims $500,000,000 is lost each year as a result of the Clean Air Act, but the method by which the Heritage Foundation calculated those numbers is unavailable. Do not accept data when you cannot reproduce the data yourself. In fact, one journal article attempted to reproduce many famous studies and ultimately concluded that "80% of published research findings are false." Insist on methodology.

If you're looking for more on statistical fallacies, there's a great free online text called "Learning Statistics Using R" that has an opening section on many statistical fallacies and standards for high-quality research.

3. Alternative Data – Respond with *Counter Research*

While response types 1 and 2 above question the logic or research of your opponents, it is advisable to respond with contradictory data. Whether historical examples, opposing research, or more recent statistics, data convinces audiences and conflicting data can make for a fascinating debate. You probably want to combine any alternative data with some other response regarding poor logic or poor research, thereby helping your alternative data shine.

Here are a few examples:

1. **UK Proves Gun Bans Fail:** My opponents told you that after the handgun ban in 1997 in the United Kingdom, the firearm homicide rate fell dramatically. But firearm homicides are just a subset of violent crime, and firearm homicides in England fluctuate wildly – having both doubled and halved in the time since the gun ban. But looking at all firearm crime reported by the British Home Office in 2000, there has been a steady increase since the gun ban. The gun ban simply made UK citizens easy prey.

2. **WWII Privacy Violations Acceptable:** War is a terrible thing. In the Second World War it was horrible that we interned Japanese Americans in internment camps. Yet, while their privacy was violated temporarily, the idea of privacy violation in war is acceptable so long as it is restored afterwards. Consider every soldier who was drafted (similar to being seized from your home), trained in boot camp (similar to being placed in a camp you cannot leave), then sent to trenches (far worse privacy violations than living in a confined space), with their mail read and ultimately being asked to give their life. This is horrible too. But it was needed. Unless you're willing to say the U.S. should not have even entered World War II, the Japanese Internment Camps example cannot stand as a reason to prioritize privacy over security.

3. **Tragedy of the Commons:** My opponent has argued that increasing environmental protections from the Government will help preserve the environment. But historically, such protections backfire because no particular person has an incentive to care for that environment. It's the same reason you don't want to buy a former rental car – nobody who drove it needed to care for it. In Dr. Terry Anderson's article "Shoot an Elephant, Save a Community" he

compares Zimbabwe and Kenya environmental regulations responding to the same problem of declining wildlife populations. In Kenya, its 1977 ban on all hunting of large wild animals led to a 60% decline in their population! But in Zimbabwe, the World Wildlife Fund helped implement a community management approach where locals actually were given ownership of the animals – including authority to allow safari hunting! "Ten years after the program began, wildlife populations had increased by 50 percent" says Dr. Anderson. Ownership, not protection, is how to help the environment survive and flourish.

For these responses, dig into your personal experience, history, statistics, books, statistics, and journal articles. Realize that **a data debate is on your opponent's turf.** To refute someone who has prepared information, you will likely have to go deeper or have some sort of special knowledge to refute with counter-data.

4. Significance – Respond to the *Importance*

The importance of arguments should be thought of as arguments on a scale, not a binary result. In other words, mitigating responses often conclude that some point is less relevant or less important, not completely irrelevant or unimportant.

There are three classic arguments to reduce the importance of someone's argument: quantitative significance, qualitative significance, and outweighing.

1. **Quantitative Significance:** Respond by showing there is no overall pattern or trend, and an isolated example does not prove an overall point. For example, when someone tells a sob story as a means of proof, you may respond by saying that what happened to one person

was horrible, but the quantification needed to make a policy change is lacking.

2. **Qualitative Significance:** Respond by showing that numerically large data doesn't demonstrate anything qualitatively meaningful. For example, when someone touts off the latest numbers on trade deficit, showing some multi-billion deficit for the USA, it's worth arguing that a trade deficit isn't harmful to an economy.

3. **Outweigh:** Outweighing is the "it's worth it" response. If your opponent argues that the Transportation Security Administration's cost of $8,000,000,000 is "costly," you may respond by saying "it's worth the security benefit" and then prove some security benefit. Outweighing, therefore, can link to your offense! You may show that deeper principles, such as a goal or value, are the benefit of the apparent harm of cost, or you may show that some disadvantage or advantage outweighs the importance of the point your opponent has made.

If that sounds confusing, think of yourself in a business meeting: the director of sales has just finished a speech against the current project schedule, saying that a competitor is going to get ahead if the company doesn't release its product ahead of schedule. The director of engineering may respond by arguing that quality would suffer so much, and the end result would be unhappy customers – which is worse than getting to market second. This response is an "outweighing" response, linking to the disadvantage of poor quality.

So why does "Outweighing" appear here in micro-refutation, when it's also in macro-refutation? The reason is because outweighing may occur with a substantial investment of time, using an offensive point like a disadvantage, or it may be a quick flick of the wrist as micro-refutation, as in "my opponents are right that there's a cost, but the benefit seems worth it to me."

Significance arguments often contain the entirety of a debate round. It's worth getting familiar with thinking through these responses. (<< that sentence is a significance point!)

5. Causal Analysis – Respond to the *Deeper Why*

If you don't know why your achilles tendon is hurting, should you start electrode therapy? Prooooobably not.

Analyzing causality is one of the most effective ways to go deeper than your opponent. If you can identify other trends or attitudes that led to the problem they've described, then you are likely going to refute the solution they have advocated. Often a communicator will say "you're just putting a Band-Aid on the issue," or "you've identified the symptom, but not the disease." Medical analogies abound for some reason when we discuss causality. Perhaps because doctors always seem to disagree about what was wrong? But we digress...

Here are a few example responses using causality.

1. **Root Cause is Poverty:** Let's imagine your opponents have decided to stop all trade with Nigeria, due to recent upticks in terrorism. You may see more deeply and argue that the root cause of the terrorism isn't that we trade with them, but it is how poverty factors into the terrorist psyche. This argument is attitudinal causality because it's about attitudes.

2. **Alternate Cause – The Powerful Media:** Let's say your opponents are debating about politics and disparaging the "ignorant electorate." You may respond by showing it is not ignorance in the educational sense that is the problem, rather it is how the media isolates and

distorts information, controlling the conversation. This argument is existential causality because it blames a problem on some trend that has developed into a barrier.

3. **The Real Problem is Who's On the Committee:** Let's say your opponents have passed a new policy managing marine resources, in response to some mismanagement by the federal agency in charge (a real case a few years back). But you looked up the U.S. Fishery Management Councils and noticed that most are composed partially of federal employees and then largely of businesspeople who have significant corporate interest. As a result, you argue the root cause isn't the policies in place, it's the structure of the council that tends towards corruption. This argument is structural causality because it's about how core structures are the root cause.

These three types of causality – attitudinal, existential, and structural – are the main types of root causes you could encounter and point out as the deeper why behind any problems. The next step of this argument can be to show how your opponent's solution does not cover the full depth of the problem, and thereby masks the problem in a way that guarantees it festers and gets worse. At that point you're in offense territory, running a disadvantage.

So causality arguments can challenge your opponent's understanding of the problem on the one hand, while turning into the root cause of a disadvantage on the other. Nice!

6. Predictive Analysis – Respond to the *Solution*

What if your opponent proposes some future change? Maybe a policy, or maybe just an implication of your opponent's philosophical stance. You may want to mitigate the solution by arguing against its effectiveness.

The key point here is to understand that both of you are making predictions about the future, and you're decreasing the strength of your opponent's prediction. In other words, you're both speculating.

Here are a few predictive arguments to prompt your refutation:

1. **Lacks Specificity:** Perhaps your opponent has said that airport security measures are too invasive of privacy. But under questioning, your opponent was unwilling to commit to a "no security" approach to air travel. You might point out that your opponent's implied solution here doesn't have enough specifics to be considered any further – how can you determine whether airport security measures are too invasive if you've got no alternative measures to compare?

2. **Non-Workable Solution:** Let's say your opponents have proposed a plan to fix the federal court system by requiring video recording of all custodial interrogations. You may point out that such a plan is not really workable in the field, where police officers may find themselves conducting a custodial interrogation outdoors in an unplanned environment like a getaway vehicle, or without electricity. A policy that doesn't think through the day-to-day of a crime fighter may risk no interrogations happening because of an overly stringent plan.

3. **Insurmountable Barriers:** One time there was a case to provide citizenship to the 300 or so kids of American Citizens in the Confederation of the Northern Mariana Islands. They should have had citizenship, but there was an accidental loophole for a few years that rendered them stateless... and nobody realized it until these kids were old enough to get driver's licenses. A barriers-based response to the solution of giving out the citizenship was the argument that the exact names of each of these stateless kids were not yet known, and

Congress had tasked a commission to figure that out before Congress was willing to pass legislation. Therefore, don't pass the plan yet because it has a barrier standing in its way: identifying the stateless kids.

Lacking specificity, workability challenges, or the inability to surpass certain barriers are three of the best types of micro-refutation arguments against solutions. Obviously, there are far more arguments against solutions, but realize that many are macro-refutation like disadvantages and counterplans. Still, casting doubt on the likely success of a plan is a strong tactic.

Whew! We have just put words to a whole bunch of things you already knew. Hopefully you're building confidence that you can do this whole debate thing, because debate simply applies your learning from other areas of life and education. Time to get out there and try it!

Conclusion

Persuasion is a method of leading an audience to a conclusion, not browbeating someone until they come to your position. It is most successful when you remove yourself as self from the equation, and ensure that there is merely a clash of ideas. You may have discovered something about certain ideas, but you're not selling yourself, you're selling the idea and ideas belong to anyone.

Making a case is the starting point for persuasive communication, but it's not the ending point. Real persuasion has a back-and-forth.

To find the crux, use the tools of stasis and shared assumptions to figure out exactly where the controversy lies. Never argue at the conclusion level when your audience does not share the assumptions that got you there!

It's time to get out there and try it.

You're cultivating a skill and mental habits that you can practice, not just ones that you can understand. That's why it's important to make sure your actual abilities keep up with your knowledge. The next section of the book will take your critical thinking and debating to the next level of depth, but requires some experience to make any sense.

Debate is more caught than taught, and you need to go catch some rounds before returning to the puddle of learning.

What's in Section 2?

Here is what you can expect after you've practiced some debating and are ready to take a deeper dive into structures, theories, and strategies. Section 2 will guide you on your journey towards master debater. Its chapters are:

- Classical Rhetoric Crash Course
- Everything Research
- Everything Proof
- The Argument Map
- Intro to Stock Issues
- Why? (Significance)
- Knowable Causes (Inherency)
- Predictive Causes (Solvency, Advantages, and Disadvantages)
- Structuring Disadvantages and Consequences
- Using Frameworks in Policy Debate
- Counterplans
- Using Metadebate
- Arguing Interpretation
- Eight Case Stuctures You Must Know
- Twenty-One Steps to a Bullet Proof Affirmative
- What to Do In Each Speech
- How to Shell & Extend

About the Authors

Isaiah McPeak

Isaiah is a tech entrepreneur by day and a debate coach by night, who specializes in helping people unlock their potential as communicators. He has coached CEOs, authors, public speakers, politicians, and business professionals in classical rhetoric and modern speaking technique. His presentations and writing have been used in Fortune 500 business summits, small business company offsites, high-stakes consulting, multi-million dollar sales pitches, education, and successful venture capital pitches. Isaiah has also delivered over 1,000 speeches and frequently speaks at events on topics of business, marketing, leadership, and communication.

In 2003, Isaiah and his now wife Amy formed a two-team debate club coached by Lisa Alexander, and the teams placed 13th and 3rd at the 2004 NCFCA national championship. Both would go on to debate in college, even partnering for a 4th place national title in NEDA in 2006. Isaiah went on to debate in team value, team policy, LD value, LD policy, American parliamentary, and moot court formats, placing in the top five nationally five separate times, and winning dozens of tournaments and first place speaker awards. He has also directed tournaments or coached in 11 leagues total.

Isaiah went on to coach the Patrick Henry College debate team, a squad of 60 debaters in multiple leagues who brought home two trophy cases of awards in three years, including a national 1st place award. But Isaiah's greatest joy comes from coaching high school students. That's where the debate bug caught him and changed his life. Isaiah and Amy have been on the founding teams of five debate clubs, and volunteer by coaching at local clubs and nonprofits.

Isaiah has personally mentored more than 50 students in the last 12 years of coaching. While he has coached several first-place national champions in various formats, what really excites Isaiah is when someone makes a giant leap of improvement after challenging self – whether winning a national championship or initiating a difficult conversation. For Isaiah, a debater succeeds by turning argumentativeness upside down and disciplining self to listen, make peace, teach, and move others towards good.

Isaiah and Amy have two daughters and live in Austin, TX.

Betsy McPeak

Betsy is known as a life-time learner. She is a Renaissance Woman – from rifle twirling to philosophy degrees, from becoming a C.S. Lewis Institute Fellow to exhibiting her watercolor paintings, from studying apologetics at Cambridge to building Prezi presentations for authors and businesses, from visiting missionaries in Africa to baking bread at home, from teaching seminars on Classical Education to coaching some of the top debaters in the USA, including her son Josiah that won both parliamentary and team policy debate national championships in his final year of high school. So it meshed with the pattern of her life when she became a debate teacher and coach in the fall of 2001, because it meant learning the art of communication along with her students.

Teaching debate gave more to Betsy than she gave in return. For example, one of her students that first year had a speech impediment. After much hard work on the student's part, he won the Best Speaker award at his first debate tournament. At the end of the tournament, the student went up to Betsy and said he felt like she should have the trophy. Awards aside, the joy of being a part of a student's growth, and even transformation, became the motivation to coach and teach for the next 15 years. The many emails Betsy has received from students who see how much the critical thinking and communication skills help them in their life beyond debate tournaments has been a great reward.

Betsy has coached and taught speech and debate, started debate clubs in Illinois and Maryland, directed debate tournaments in Maryland and Virginia, taught debate camps from New Jersey to Utah, judged a gazillion debate rounds, designed presentations for CEOs and coached them through the delivery of keynote speeches, and personally coached many who make a living by speaking on some platform, including poets, workshop teachers, politicians, and pastors.

Betsy likes to travel, paint, and read. She lives near Annapolis, Maryland with her best friend of 35 years, her husband David.